Terror Attack Brighton

The Grand Hotel, Brighton.

'An evil group has once again planned and carried out an attack on innocent people in pursuit of their aims. They have deliberately struck at the heart of our nation'

Deputy Prime Minister Willie Whitelaw
in the House of Lords, a few days after the explosion

'Total security is impossible in a free, democratic society, but in the light of Brighton we must enhance previously acceptable levels of security'

Home Secretary, Leon Brittan,
three months after the Brighton bomb

Terror Attack Brighton

Blowing Up the Iron Lady

Kieran Hughes

PEN & SWORD
POLITICS

First published in Great Britain in 2014 by
Pen & Sword Politics
an imprint of
Pen & Sword Books Ltd
47 Church Street
Barnsley
South Yorkshire
S70 2AS

ISBN 978 1 47382 329 7

A CIP catalogue record for this book is available from the British
Library

Typeset in Ehrhardt by
Mac Style Ltd, Bridlington, East Yorkshire
Printed and bound in the UK by CPI Group (UK) Ltd,
Croydon, CRO 4YY

Pen & Sword Books Ltd incorporates the imprints of Pen & Sword
Archaeology, Atlas, Aviation, Battleground, Discovery, Family
History, History, Maritime, Military, Naval, Politics, Railways,
Select, Transport, True Crime, and Fiction, Frontline Books, Leo
Cooper, Praetorian Press, Seaforth Publishing and Wharncliffe.

For a complete list of Pen & Sword titles please contact
PEN & SWORD BOOKS LIMITED
47 Church Street, Barnsley, South Yorkshire, S70 2AS, England
E-mail: enquiries@pen-and-sword.co.uk
Website: www.pen-and-sword.co.uk

Dedication

This book is dedicated to my Mum and her brave fight against cancer ... a real inspiration, and to those who died or who suffered terribly as a result of the Brighton bombing.

The five people killed in the bombing were:

Sir Anthony Berry, 59, the MP for Enfield Southgate
Roberta Wakeham, 45, wife of the then Tory Chief Whip Lord Wakeham
Eric Taylor, 54, the Tories' North West Area Chairman
Muriel Maclean, 54, wife of the President of the Scottish Conservatives,
    Sir Donald Maclean
Jeanne Shattock, 52, wife of the Tories' Western Area Chairman

Margaret Tebbit was permanently paralysed in the attack

Contents

Acknowledgements

I am grateful to a number of individuals who have assisted my research over the years, from the project's inception as an undergraduate dissertation to its release as a book five years later. Not least my interviewees at undergraduate level who gave up their time to help me and inspire my interest in this topic. My thanks go to Lord Tebbit, George Hammond, Lord Stockton, Canon Robert Fayers – and Jo Berry who organised my original meeting with Patrick Magee that led to a deeper interest in the bombing but also the troubles in Northern Ireland. I am grateful to Patrick for speaking candidly with me during my time as a history graduate at the University of Reading. My other thanks in later research go to Chief Constable Simon Parr, staff at The Keep in Brighton, Lord Jenkin, Simon Fanshawe and Jon Orrell. My usual thanks for their continued support go to the staff at Pen and Sword Publishing, especially Lisa Hooson, editor Alison Miles and my agent Hilary Elston. It was my Mum who really got me into gear to write this book and without her I would probably have started writing it in time for the fiftieth anniversary!

Thanks to my historical consultant Phil Seaman for checking my work and offering advice and making corrections. Thanks also to Hugh Mothersole for his assistance in IT matters. Any errors or omissions that remain are therefore my own. My sincere thanks go to my family in general who have supported me during the very busy time putting this book together – sorry I ignored you at the time. Thanks to Nabeela for looking after me when I was ill during the time that I was researching and writing this book. Thanks, once again, to Nikki and Tim at TCS Autos in High Wycombe for keeping me motoring during the busy days of researching and writing. Your support is very much appreciated.

In the book I have attempted to compile a narrative of events with some analysis of the twists and turns from the time, as well as my own opinions and theories. However, it is not my intention to sympathise or support any particular political side and I have tried to stay neutral, while examining ideas, contributions and reactions from different political angles at all times. Intentionally, I have attempted to examine the wider situation surrounding the Brighton bombing by looking at the Troubles leading up to the explosion, as well as the investigation, trial, albeit briefly, and subsequent security issues. I have used some of the newly released archive material but made the decision to be quite selective and have left out some of the documents that I felt were repetitive. I hope you enjoy the book; I have been given access to some very interesting interviewees and primary sources to put together a contextualised account of what happened, as well as exploring the emotions, reactions and impact of the bombing. Further reading on this topic from me can be found at www. yellowboxhistory.co.uk.

Chapter 1

Key Characters

Some of these people feature heavily in the book, some not so heavily and there are a few that did not make it in to the final draft but still need to be mentioned.

Gerry Adams

Born in 1948, Gerry Adams has been a senior Sinn Fein figure for several decades, vice-president, president and MP. Sinn Fein is the political wing of the IRA. Adams states that he has never been a member of the Provisional Irish Republican Army (IRA). However, a number of former members have accused him of being a member in the past. Adams has called these comments 'libellous' and insists that he has never been a member of the IRA but neither has he ever disassociated himself from it.

Robert Armstrong

Born in 1927, Armstrong was educated at Eton College and Oxford University, later becoming a successful civil servant. From 1979 to 1987, he served as Secretary of the Cabinet under Margaret Thatcher.

Fred Bishop

Bishop was a station officer with the East Sussex Fire Brigade in 1984. He was the fireman who pulled Norman Tebbit out of the rubble. He asked Tebbit if he was okay and Tebbit yelled at him to get off his foot! Bishop made the decision to go into the hotel against procedure (if a bomb explodes) because he knew people were trapped and needed help quickly.

Anthony Berry

Sir Anthony Berry was the MP for Southgate and one of the five people who died when the Grand Hotel, Brighton was ripped apart by a bomb on 12 October 1984. The 59-year-old had been staying in a room below the explosion and was killed in the blast.

Jo Berry

The daughter of Anthony Berry and the Hon. Mary Roche, an aunt of Diana, Princess of Wales. Her father Anthony Berry was killed in the explosion. Berry met Patrick Magee in November 2000, in an effort to work at reconciliation. They now tour together to promote dialogue and understanding of conflict and resolution.

Leon Brittan

Born in 1939, Leon Brittan is a barrister turned MP, as well as a former Home Secretary in the earlier Thatcher years. During the miners' strike of 1984–5, he accused the NUM of organising violence by using flying pickets. In 1985, Brittan was moved to Secretary of State for Trade and Industry. He was created Baron Brittan of Spennithorne in 2000. He reported to Parliament on the ongoing investigation into the Brighton bombing and the findings of the Hoddinott Report into security at the hotel and conference.

Cynthia Crawford

She became a close friend, personal assistant and confidante of Margaret Thatcher, helping to run her household throughout her time as Prime Minister. She was nicknamed 'Crawfie' by the Thatchers. Crawford was with the Thatchers on the night of the Brighton bombing and can be seen in several photos leaving the scene of the explosion with them in a car. She spent time with Margaret Thatcher throughout that morning, reflecting and praying.

Michael Dobbs

Born in 1948, Dobbs has never had a proper job his website says, tongue in cheek. However, following a long career in politics he became a member of the House of Lords as Lord Dobbs of Wylye, in 2010, sitting as a Conservative peer. He had previously been Chief of Staff and later Deputy Chairman of the Conservative Party. He was an advisor to Margaret Thatcher when she was leader of the Opposition from 1975 to 1979. Dobbs held a number of key posts in the 1980s and 1990s. From 1981 to 1986 he was a government special advisor. Then he was appointed the Conservative Party Chief of Staff from 1986 to 1987. He was with Margaret Thatcher when she entered Downing Street as Prime Minister, and he was with John Major when he was voted out. He was bombed in Brighton in 1984 and fell out with Margaret Thatcher so badly at one point that he was actually banished from Chequers. In John Major's government he served as Deputy Chairman of the Conservative Party from 1994 to 1995.

Colonel Muammar Gaddafi

The former Libyan leader was born in 1942 and was assassinated in 2011. He seized power from King Idris in 1969 and became one of the longest serving leaders in the region. He was often regarded as a ruthless dictator who ruled with an iron fist, repressive, violent and abusive. In the West, Gaddafi was often associated with terrorism, accused of supporting groups such as FARC in Colombia and the IRA in Northern Ireland. In 1986 the United States launched air attacks on Tripoli and Benghazi in retaliation for Libya's alleged involvement in the bombing of a Berlin nightclub and the subsequent deaths of two American soldiers. As a result of the raids, thirty-five Libyans were killed, including Gaddafi's adopted daughter (some claim that she is still alive). Gaddafi was also behind the 1988 bombing of the Pan Am flight over Lockerbie in Scotland and paid out millions of dollars to American victims' families. Campaigners spent years trying to achieve this goal. Gaddafi was blamed for training and supplying some IRA terrorists.

Roy Hattersley

Born in 1932, Hattersley was an MP from 1964 to 1997. Some of the posts he has held include: Shadow Secretary of State, 1987–92, Shadow Chancellor of the Exchequer, 1983–7 and Deputy Leader of the Labour Party, 1983–92. The Rt Hon. the Lord Hattersley joined the House of Lords on 24 November 1997.

(Lord) Jenkin of Roding, formerly (Charles) Patrick Jenkin

This Cambridge-educated barrister, turned councillor became MP for Wanstead and Woodford in 1964. In 1974 he became Minister for Energy and later served under Margaret Thatcher as Secretary of State for Health and Social Security, then Industry and later Environment. In 1987 he was elevated to the House of Lords as Baron Jenkin of Roding. He was a guest at the Grand Hotel on 12 October 1984, and was in a single room at the back of the hotel as his wife was not with him on that occasion. After the explosion, he escaped wearing a raincoat and nothing underneath it. Marks & Spencer came to his rescue to preserve his dignity.

Lord McAlpine

Robert Alistair McAlpine, Baron McAlpine of West Green (b. 1942, d. 2014), was a British businessman and politician who was an advisor to Prime Minister Margaret Thatcher. He became prominent in politics in the 1980s as the treasurer and fundraiser of the Conservative Party. He served as Deputy Chairman of the Conservative Party from 1979 to 1983 and treasurer from 1975 to 1990. He was an early supporter of Margaret Thatcher and was considered by many as the most successful fundraiser the party ever had, although he never became a significant political figure.

He was at the Grand Hotel the night the bomb exploded and had held one of his parties the night before. After the bombing he used his business connections to get Marks & Spencer to open early so delegates could dress smartly before the conference resumed. Many had lost their clothes in the explosion and it was Thatcher's absolute determination that the conference would go on, without delay.

Martin McGuinness

The Mid-Ulster Sinn Fein Member of the Legislative Assembly (MLA) was born in 1950. The Sinn Fein website says he became involved in the Civil Rights Movement after 5 October 1968 and joined Sinn Fein in 1970.

Donald Maclean

The optician turned MP, and President of the Scottish Conservatives, was thrown against a wall in the blast and then fell two storeys but was still alive by the time fire and rescue personnel found him. His wife also survived the explosion, but died five weeks later from her injuries. He died in May 2010, aged 79, having survived the Brighton bombing despite the device, intended for Margaret Thatcher, having been planted in his bathroom. He was knighted in 1985 and recovered to give evidence at the Old Bailey during the trial of Patrick Magee and four others for carrying out the bombing in Brighton.

Muriel Maclean

Muriel was the wife of the President of the Scottish Conservative Association, Donald Maclean. Colleagues spoke of her bravery as she fought for her life in hospital for more than four weeks after the blast. The Macleans had been staying in Room 629 where the bomb had been planted. On 14 November 1984 the *Glasgow Herald* ran its headline 'Fifth

Brighton Hotel Victim is Dead'. Dr Skidmore and an ambulance man gave Mrs Maclean first aid on the sixth floor after the explosion before she was transferred to a stretcher and taken to hospital.

Patrick Magee

The Brighton bomber who was given eight life sentences for killing five members of the Conservative Party. He now travels around the world lecturing on peace and reconciliation. Magee was freed from jail in 1999 as part of the Good Friday Agreement after serving fourteen years in prison. He has formed a working relationship with Jo Berry, the daughter of one of the victims of the bombing, Sir Anthony Berry.

Brighton bomber, Patrick Magee.
(Photo: Kieran Hughes)

Danny Morrison

Morrison is a writer who lives in West Belfast. In the 1980s he was the national director of publicity for Sinn Fein, and has served time as an IRA prisoner and been a regular political commentator in the press. He was a Sinn Fein press officer when the voices of those the UK government suspected of supporting terrorism were banned across the country's media. During the 1981 hunger strikes he was a spokesperson for Bobby Sands MP. He was elected in Mid-Ulster to the Northern Ireland Assembly on an abstentionist ticket in October 1982.

Brian Murray

Murray, who died in 2013, was part of the first of the ambulance crews to arrive at the scene. He raced in to help others before he had even finished putting on his safety equipment. Lord Tebbit paid tribute to the kindness of the man and thinks it was Murray whom he told he was allergic to bombs. Murray also pulled Chief Whip John Wakeman and MP Sir Walter Clegg to safety. He was awarded the British Empire Medal for his bravery. The Queen and the Prime Minister also sent personal messages to him acknowledging his bravery that night, having rescued several people and bringing them to the front area of the hotel so they could be taken to hospital. He spent hours dodging live electrical wires and dripping water.

Airey Neave

Airey Neave (b. 1916, d. 1979) was a war hero and the first Englishman to escape from Colditz. His political life later saw him serve as Shadow Secretary of State for Northern Ireland. According to Brian Harrison, before Margaret Thatcher even became Conservative Party leader, Neave told her that Northern Ireland was the only portfolio he wanted.[1] He was MP for Abingdon from 1953 until his death. He was assassinated by the Irish National Liberation Army (INLA) in March 1979 in the House of Commons car park, and died an hour after being freed from his car. This was a month before Margaret Thatcher became Prime Minister. Airey Neave and Margaret Thatcher had a very close working relationship, and he was one of her key advisors after she was elected as leader of the Conservative Party in 1975.

Airey Neave. *(Photo: courtesy of aireyneavetrust.org)*

Sean O'Callaghan

O'Callaghan is a former head of the IRA Southern Command and author of *The Informer*. He left the IRA in his early twenties and became an informer for the UK government. He turned against the IRA after the murder of Lord Mountbatten, in which several children died. O'Callaghan has spent time in prisons in England and Ireland and now, as a free man, speaks out openly against the IRA.

Chief Constable Simon Parr (Cambridgeshire Police)

Chief Constable of Cambridgeshire Police, Simon Parr was one of the first police officers to arrive at the scene of the bombing, as he was a police constable serving in Brighton at the time. Parr spent twenty years with Sussex Police and was commander of the East Downs Division. He became head of the Operations Department and thus was in charge of handling many major incidents and events, notably the public order policing of several conferences in Brighton.

Chief Constable Simon Parr (Cambridgeshire Police). *(Photo courtesy of Cambridgeshire Police)*

Michael Portillo

Michael Portillo was born in North London in 1953. A Cambridge history graduate, he joined the Conservative Research Department in 1975, where he spent three years. Portillo unsuccessfully contested the Birmingham Perry Bar seat at the 1983 election. In December 1984 he won the Enfield Southgate by-election following the murder of Sir Anthony Berry, in the bombing at the Grand Hotel.

Charles Powell

Born in 1941, Powell joined the Her Majesty's Diplomatic Service after graduating from university in 1963. After a number of posts abroad he returned to the UK to work at the Foreign and Commonwealth Office. He was seconded to 10 Downing Street and served as Private Secretary to Margaret Thatcher from 1983 to 1990. In later years he served John Major in the same role.

Gordon Shattock

Born in 1928, Shattock cheated death on the night of the Brighton bombing, despite being in Room 628, but his wife Jeanne was one of five fatalities. Gordon was the Conservative Party's Western Area Chairman. In the 1985 Birthday Honours Gordon Shattock received a knighthood, as well as Donald Maclean, President of the Scottish Conservatives, who also survived the bomb attack but lost his wife. Sir Gordon remarried in 1988 and died in April 2010.

Jeanne Shattock

Jeanne Shattock, aged 52, was one of the fatalities of the explosion. The Shattocks were staying in room 628 and she was in the bathroom when the bomb went off. She was forced through the corridor in the blast, through several toppling walls at great speed, into room 638, where she died.

Eric Taylor

He was the North-West Area Chairman of the Tories and in the room directly below Sir Anthony Berry. The Oldham-born politician served on Oldham Council from 1961 to 1974 and as a magistrate from 1966. In 1974 he was awarded the OBE for services to politics. He died in the bombing.

Margaret Tebbit

Margaret, later Lady Tebbit (Norman's wife), was seriously injured in the explosion and left with permanent paralysing injuries. She showed great courage in the years that followed and was always supported by her husband and their friends.

Norman Tebbit

Norman Tebbit is a British Conservative politician, a former Member of Parliament for Chingford and senior Cabinet minister under Margaret Thatcher. He was Employment Secretary, 1981–3, Trade and Industry Secretary, 1983–5 and Tory Chairman, 1985–7. The iconic photographs of him being pulled out of the rubble at the Grand Hotel hours after the explosion were part of history in the making. He was later made Lord Tebbit.

(Lord) Norman Tebbit in the House of Lords lobby, 2009. *(Photo: Kieran Hughes)*

Denis Thatcher

The role of Denis Thatcher has sometimes been underestimated. According to Denis himself, his role was to support his wife during a long and sometimes difficult premiership. Christopher Collins has stated that one of his roles was to boost her confidence which he says was 'not as unshakeable as most assumed'.[2] Collins insists that Margaret Thatcher 'would not have functioned politically at such a high level, and for as long as she did, without him'.[3] He was one of the first to realise the political significance of the resignation of Geoffrey Howe in November 1990. Denis was in Margaret's suite when the explosion went off, was taken out of the hotel with her, was the only person with her soon after and provided support in the months that followed. She was personally and politically shaken by events and if Lord Stockton is correct, her confidence was shaken by the IRA's 'we only have to be lucky once' statement (see p. 48), then Denis played a bigger part in keeping her on track over the coming months than anyone has ever given him credit for.

Harvey Thomas

The former Tory director of presentation and a senior advisor to Mrs Thatcher said he felt it was important to forgive the Brighton bomber. He says that he made the decision to meet and forgive him because it was an important part of his religion. He was blown through the roof and fell several floors after the explosion.

John Wakeham

John Wakeham, Baron Wakeham (b. 1932) is a businessman and British Conservative Party politician. He was first elected to the House of Commons in 1974. He became a minister after Margaret Thatcher's victory in 1979. His first wife, Roberta, was killed in the Brighton hotel bombing and he was trapped in the rubble for seven hours. During the late 1980s he served as Leader of the House of Commons. He was appointed a life peer as Baron Wakeham of Maldon in the County of Essex in 1992.

Roberta Wakeham

A plaque in St Paul's Church, West Street, Brighton pays tribute to John Wakeham's wife who died in the Brighton bombing and the other losses. It reads: 'In proud memory. Anthony Berry, Muriel Maclean, Jeanne Shattock, Eric Taylor and Roberta Wakeham who died in the Brighton bombing October 12th 1984. They paid the price of Freedom. Requiescant in Peace.'[4]

The plaque in St Paul's Church in memory of those who died; it is to the right of the door. *(Photo: courtesy of St. Paul's Church)*

Chapter 2

Thatcher's Men – the Cabinet, June 1983–June 1987

- Margaret Thatcher – Prime Minister
- Lord Whitelaw – Deputy Prime Minister and Lord President of the Council
- Lord Hailsham of St Marylebone – Lord Chancellor
- John Biffen – Lord Privy Seal
- Nigel Lawson – Chancellor of the Exchequer
- Peter Rees – Chief Secretary to the Treasury
- Sir Geoffrey Howe – Secretary of State for Foreign and Commonwealth Affairs
- Leon Brittan – Secretary of State for the Home Department
- Michael Jopling – Minister of Agriculture, Fisheries and Food
- Michael Heseltine – Secretary of State for Defence
- Sir Keith Joseph – Secretary of State for Education and Science
- Norman Tebbit – Secretary of State for Employment
- Peter Walker – Secretary of State for Energy
- Patrick Jenkin – Secretary of State for the Environment
- Norman Fowler – Secretary of State for Health
- Lord Cockfield – Chancellor of the Duchy of Lancaster
- James Prior – Secretary of State for Northern Ireland
- George Younger – Secretary of State for Scotland
- Cecil Parkinson – Secretary of State for Trade and Industry
- Tom King – Secretary of State for Transport
- Nicholas Edwards – Secretary of State for Wales
- John Wakeham – Chief Whip

Some of the Main Changes at that Time

October 1983: Tom King succeeded Norman Tebbit as Secretary of State for Employment. Norman Tebbit took over from Cecil Parkinson as Secretary of State for Trade and Industry. Nicholas Ridley replaced Tom King as Secretary of State for Transport.

September 1984: Lord Gowrie succeeded Lord Cockfield as Chancellor of the Duchy of Lancaster. Douglas Hurd took over from James Prior as Secretary of State for Northern Ireland. Lord Young of Graffham entered the Cabinet as Minister without Portfolio.

January 1986: Malcolm Rifkind replaced George Younger as Secretary of State for Scotland. Younger took over from Michael Heseltine as Secretary of State for Defence.

January 1986: Paul Channon replaced Leon Brittan as Secretary of State for Trade and Industry.

Chapter 3

Northern Ireland Secretaries

Having looked briefly at the people in the public eye at the time of the bombing, it is also necessary to understand the political context. The next few pages will look at the background and events leading up to the explosion. To offer full contextualisation, the book will also examine events after the bombing to be able to put the Good Friday Agreement in the right place.

In Northern Ireland today, the once-powerful Secretary of State with a massive political portfolio is now limited to representing the interests of the people in Cabinet meetings. He or she oversees the devolved administration but is still responsible for a number of key issues such as security, administration of elections and human rights. The Secretary of State for Wales and Secretary of State for Scotland usually represent a constituency from there but it has been different in Northern Ireland, with no Labour candidates fielded in the North and no Conservative representation on the Assembly.

Before 1972 it was the Home Secretary who was in charge of matters concerning Northern Ireland. This can be seen by the UK government's reaction to serious civil disobedience and Home Secretary James Callaghan's orders to send in the British army to the province in 1969. The office of Secretary of State for Northern Ireland was created after the abolition of the Northern Ireland Parliament. The UK government had become seriously worried that the Northern Ireland government (at Stormont) was losing control. In March 1972 it announced that direct rule from Westminster would be introduced. Since 1972 a series of Northern Ireland Secretaries have taken control but with diminished powers in recent years. As recently as 2010 further powers in relation to justice and policing were given to the Assembly.

Northern Ireland Secretaries Since 1972

- William Whitelaw, March 1972–December 1973 (Conservative)
- Francis Pym, December 1973–March 1974 (Conservative)
- Merlyn Rees, March 1974–September 1976 (Labour)
- Roy Mason, September 1976–May 1979 (Labour)
- Humphrey Atkins, May 1979–September 1981 (Conservative)
- James Prior, September 1981–September 1984 (Conservative)
- Douglas Hurd, September 1984–September 1985 (Conservative)
- Tom King, September 1985–July 1989 (Conservative)
- Peter Brooke, July 1989–April 1992 (Conservative)
- Sir Patrick Mayhew, April 1992–May 1997 (Conservative)
- Mo Mowlam, May 1997–October 1999 (Labour)

Mowlam was the first woman to take up the post of Northern Ireland Secretary when Prime Minister Tony Blair appointed her. She was successful in helping to restore an IRA ceasefire and for encouraging all sides to negotiate and participate in talks. She included Sinn Fein in multi-party talks and went in person to the Maze Prison to talk to Ulster Loyalists to persuade them to take part in the peace process. She went unaccompanied and sat and talked to potentially dangerous men.

- Peter Mandelson, October 1999–January 2001 (Labour)
- John Reid, January 2001–October 2002 (Labour)
- Paul Murphy, October 2002–May 2005 (Labour)
- Peter Hain, May 2005–June 2007 (Labour)
- Shaun Woodward, June 2007–May 2010 (Labour)
- Owen Paterson, May 2010–September 2012 (Conservative)
- Theresa Villiers, September 2012– (Conservative)

Chapter 4

The Political Background, Self-rule, the Troubles and Reasons for Hatred

It is very difficult to take several hundred years of history and condense it into a few pages, while attempting to remain impartial and non-judgmental. During my research I have met people from both sides and carried out a number of lengthy discussions. I have had some interesting telephone calls and exchanged a number of emails. I have attempted to put aside my own political beliefs and present the entire story. By doing this I have a better chance of offering the full picture. The Dutch historian Leopold Von Ranke was a great believer in gathering all the evidence and telling the story from beginning to end without too much analysis, thus presenting all the facts and allowing others to analyse. His critics, such as historian E.H. Carr, pointed out that this method allows the historian enough flexibility to edit out the sources he or she wants, therefore offering a distorted and biased view of history, either wittingly or unwittingly. As an historian, I take the side of Von Ranke, but have tried not to allow my personal judgment to colour the account or by knowingly adding or taking away vital facts. I have spent time with people from both sides: Pat Magee, Norman Tebbit and those involved in the rescue operation. Many of these meetings took place during my days as an undergraduate when I first started researching the Brighton bombing. Some years later as I write this book, as part of a PhD, I have added more accounts from other politicians and people involved from all sides.

Between 1801 and 1922 Ireland was part of the United Kingdom but Anglo-Irish relations were often poor. There were many rebellions including those in 1803, 1848, 1867 and 1916. In 1886 the first attempt to legislate Home Rule was made by Gladstone's Liberal government. The move was backed by Charles Stewart Parnell's Irish Parliamentary Party. The Home Rule Bill was defeated and a second attempt in 1893 came closer when it got through the House of Commons but was later defeated in the House of Lords. Not everyone in Ireland wanted Home Rule. Unionists, so-called because of their loyalty to the 1801 Union, wanted rule from London. There was an Irish War of Independence (1919–21) and it was not until the fourth and final Home Rule Bill (the Government of Ireland Act 1920) that Ireland was partitioned into *Northern Ireland*, which was six north-eastern counties, and *Southern Ireland*, which was the rest of the island. Unionists had been allowed to opt out of the new Home Rule plan. Home Rule and an independent Southern Ireland came into force in 1922. Religion underpinned much of the sentiment in Ireland but poverty, privilege and property (land) had become the driving force by the nineteenth century. The Fenian Movement in Ireland and other places demanded independence from British rule. Some went as far as accusing the British government of genocide for failing to assist during the Great Famine. The Fenians promised to fight for independence and in 1848 a group of revolutionaries known as Young Ireland launched an unsuccessful uprising against the government. Its leaders escaped to Paris. One of them formed a new organisation called the Fenian Brotherhood in the United States. The name 'Fenians' quickly became an umbrella description to cover all the groups who wanted independence for Ireland. Many were prepared to use violence and were forced to remain secret. However, disorganisation, internal splits and lack of support from the influential Catholic priests diminished their effectiveness, support and solidarity. The demand for independence continued well into the next century.

Between 1922 and 1968 Unionists dominated politics in Northern Ireland. They ran the powerful Northern Ireland Parliament. The mainly Protestant majority of Unionists and Loyalists were often at loggerheads with the mainly Catholic minority of Nationalists and Republicans. Catholics were often discriminated against and there were riots, protests and civil unrest. Tensions increased and Catholic homes and businesses were attacked. British troops were sent in to restore order in 1969. 'Operation Banner' became the longest continuous campaign in the history of the British army, finishing in July 2007. It had only been intended as a temporary measure.

Bloody Sunday took place on 30 January 1972 in Derry, Northern Ireland, when twenty-six civil rights protesters and bystanders were shot by soldiers of the British army. As a result, thirteen males died immediately or soon after. Another man died four-and-a-half months later and his death was blamed on the injuries he received that day. The soldiers involved in the shooting were members of the First Battalion of the Parachute Regiment (1 Para). Following the deaths on Bloody Sunday there was an increase in support for the Provisional IRA. Later in 1972 the British government suspended the authority of the Northern Ireland Parliament and imposed direct rule from London. The Troubles refer to conflict between 5 October 1968 and the signing of the Good Friday Agreement on 8 April 1998. This thirty-year conflict was more about territory and national identity rather than religion and previous acrimony between Catholics and Protestants. During the 1970s the British became increasingly active in Northern Ireland. The IRA organised a bombing campaign in Ireland and mainland Britain. Bombs went off in places such as Dublin, Guildford, Woolwich, Monaghan and Birmingham. Civilians were killed and injured. From 1974 the Prevention of Terrorism Act allowed suspects to be detained without charge for up to seven days. Over the thirty-year period 169 Loyalist paramilitaries were killed, 396 Republican paramilitaries, 1,114 British security forces personnel and 1,841 civilians. Around 50,000 injuries were sustained as well.

In 1976 the British government took away 'special prisoner status' for those imprisoned for political acts. Prisoners refused to wear prison clothes and wrapped themselves in blankets. The 'dirty protest' saw prisoners smear excrement on the walls of their cells. Hunger strikes followed these unsuccessful protests and in 1981 Bobby Sands was the first hunger striker to die. Sands started his hunger strike on 1 March 1981 and died on 5 May. In total, ten hunger strikers died during the protest. As a result, support for the political wing of the Provisional IRA again increased considerably. As John Blundell stated in *Margaret Thatcher: A Portrait of the Iron Lady*, it was at this point that she became the IRA's number one target.[1] Former IRA man Sean O'Callaghan said in relation to the reaction of the death of Bobby Sands, 'she totally became a target, I mean, once she had allowed these guys to die she just became a hate figure for Republicans on a scale we hadn't seen since Cromwell'.[2] Protestors took to the streets and one typical banner stated 'Thatcher murdered Bobby Sands'. Her response was, 'it would seem dead hunger strikers who'd extinguished their own lives are of more use to the Provisional IRA then living members. Such is their cold, calculating cynicism.'[3] The deceased hunger strikers are still regarded as martyrs in Republican circles. After her death in April 2013, Sinn Fein President Gerry Adams referred to Thatcher's 'shameful' role in the hunger strikes. There were other reasons that Thatcher was becoming a bigger hate figure at the time of the bombing. Unemployment was high and the miners were on strike. Britain had become a battleground as Thatcher tried to break the dominance of the trade unions. Even thirty years after many mining communities had shut down there was evidence of hatred of the Iron Lady in some of those areas. But hatred often runs on all sides of political conflict. For example, one serving soldier told me that as a young 19-year-old, just a few weeks out of basic training, he was sent to Northern Ireland. He was in a troop of 120 men with riot shields when 10,000 Catholic marchers banging drums walked towards them. Gerry Adams was at the helm, stopped in front of this soldier and shouted in his face that he was a killer. The soldier, who had never killed anyone, said Adams shouted to him and spit was flying out. Private Danny (not his real name) said he knew through intelligence that some of the 'thugs' (his words) behind Adams were armed.

By 1983 it was supposedly Sean O'Callaghan's job to kill Prince Charles and Princess Diana. IRA commander turned informer, O'Callaghan claims to have prevented these deaths. But Danny Morrison, former Sinn

Fein director of publicity, claims O'Callaghan suggested the assassination of Charles and Diana and that the IRA rejected this. In the early 1980s IRA command told him to stay away from Patrick Magee, though, who was in the north of England and had been, it seemed, under surveillance for quite some time. O'Callaghan was shown a picture of Magee and warned that both their covers could be blown if they were seen together. Magee had been sent to Blackpool to blow up an army barracks but had pulled out of the job because of surveillance, suspecting that he was being watched and was about to be caught. However, it was here that Thatcher was seen giving her conference speech and an idea was conceived to attack her at a future party conference where they could guarantee she would be. The IRA discussed this at the highest level and the operation was given the go-ahead after careful consideration. It was finally approved in 1983 and planned for Brighton the following year despite concerns of a tremendous backlash against them if they actually succeeded in assassinating Margaret Thatcher. Sources claim that the final decision was made in a room above an unassuming bar in Carrickmore, County Tyrone.

The Brighton bombing in 1984 was one of many of the violent attacks on the British government by the IRA. Danny Morrison, also author and journalist, stated in his article 'The Price They Paid' (published in 2007), 'the bombing sent a grim message to the establishment that there was a heavy price to be paid for oppressing people … the bombing was a direct response to 1981, the hunger strike and what our community experienced under Thatcher'.[4] Morrison said he expanded and explained the thinking behind these remarks in a two-part BBC *Panorama* programme in 2007 but all of this was disappointingly edited out. Danny Morrison's article explains how he felt that the British media perpetuated the stereotypical Irish fighter in a sectarian squabble that was irrational and could not be solved. Morrison claims that this one-side presentation put forward by government and media allowed successive UK governments to issue curfew areas, torture prisoners, shoot demonstrators and hold Nationalists in prison without charge. These, along with the hunger strikes, fuelled a hatred towards the British government. He talked about feelings of anger and frustration that legitimised their emotions.

Chapter 5

Direct Rule Returns

There were growing tensions and violence between the Nationalist and Republican communities in 1968 and there were several interventions from London. This section deals with the talking and negotiating that eventually led to peace.

By 1969 the situation was so serious that order had to be restored and the British troops were sent in. By 1972 the violence had escalated so much that direct rule from Westminster was put into force. The Provisional Irish Republican Army was the main Republican paramilitary organisation in Northern Ireland at this time and wanted Irish unification and the withdrawal of British troops. In 1969 these Provisionals had broken away from the official IRA. There were secret talks between both sides in 1972 but they collapsed and the IRA organised a war of attrition to beat the British. The Ulster Defence Association (UDA) and the Ulster Volunteer Force (UVF) were Loyalist paramilitary organisations and were determined to prevent the Republicans from achieving their goal of Irish unification, even if it meant violence.

Direct rule from Westminster was not a long-term solution and by 1973 non-extremists from both sides attempted to negotiate their way around the Sunningdale Agreement. This encompassed a three-way power strategy, with input from a devolved, power-sharing administration but with the added 'Irish dimension' which meant an input from the South. Some parties refused to take part in the negotiations; others, such as extremists, were not allowed to attend. Sunningdale was a complete failure and achieved nothing. However, it showed that talking at a high level was possible and that peace was negotiable, allowing for the much more successful Good Friday Agreement twenty-five years later.

Further efforts to reach a settlement were made following increased violence after the collapse of the Sunningdale Agreement. After the Brighton bombing came the Anglo–Irish Agreement (AIA) in 1985. Not all parties supported the idea of this Agreement. Not all individual politicians were behind it either. The 'Irish question' lay at the heart of this; how much say would the South have in the running of the North? This agreement allowed for the Irish government to have an advisory role in the running of Northern Ireland, but nothing more. The Agreement made it clear that only the people could decide on Northern Ireland's constitutional future. However, the treaty alienated some of the Unionist community, which opposed Irish involvement and rejected the proposal for a devolved, power-sharing government. Thatcher infuriated the Unionists who should have been her allies. They hated the fact that the Republic of Ireland had a bigger say after the signing of the Agreement. The Revd Ian Paisley led protestors dressed in Union flags through the streets and he gave his famous 'never, never, never, never' speech, angered by the Agreement allowing the Irish Republic such as say. He asked the crowds in front of Belfast City Hall, 'Where do the terrorists operate from? From the Irish Republic! Where do the terrorists return to for sanctuary? To the Irish Republic! And yet Mrs Thatcher tells us that the Republic must have some say in our Province. We say never, never, never, never!' It is estimated that up to 200,000 people stood listening to the speech in Belfast. A few days after the speech was delivered, Ian Paisley compared Thatcher to 'Jezebel who sought to destroy Israel in a day' – speaking to his congregation.[1] Paisley wrote a letter to Thatcher accusing her of helping the IRA achieve their goal of having a united Ireland, claiming Ulster Unionists were being sacrificed on 'the altar of political expediency to appease the Dublin wolves'.[2] The Agreement was signed on 15 November 1985 and on 26 November Margaret Thatcher made some assurances to the House of Commons:

1. It was not a slippery slope to a unified Ireland.
2. There would not be a case of listening to the South and its government but not the Unionists.
3. Unionists' desire to stay part of the United Kingdom would not be ignored.
4. Greater security cooperation between the North and South.
5. Possible establishment of an Anglo-Irish inter-parliamentary body.

Sinn Fein was largely opposed to the Agreement as well but continued with the 'armalite and the ballot box' strategy. This meant a two-pronged simultaneous attack on the British presence in Northern Ireland. The IRA would head up the armed struggle, while Sinn Fein contested Northern Ireland's elections.

By 1994 many people on both sides viewed the war as unwinnable, and agreed that it could not be fought out with one side the clear victor. Both sides put themselves in a position where they could negotiate peace, or at least be involved in peace discussions. One could argue that cross-party talks began in earnest in 1996. The United States President Bill Clinton appointed veteran American senator George Mitchell as chair of the talks process. This eventually led to the Good Friday Agreement and power-sharing. For some, dealing with who they saw as terrorists was too much. Ian Paisley's Democratic Unionist Party (DUP), for example, abandoned the talks but still took their seats in the Northern Ireland Assembly.

The fragile power-sharing agreement was pushed to its limits and the disagreements over the decommissioning of arms became a major sticking point. Direct rule was imposed once again, from 2002 to 2007. The Good Friday Agreement was a huge change in the political landscape of a country in turmoil but the ballot box had triumphed over the bullet and politicians and former paramilitaries were now working again side by side when the new Assembly opened at Stormont. However, they agreed that for a change in the constitution and issues relating to the long-term governance of Northern Ireland, majorities on both sides of the border would have to agree and that referendums on the changes would have to take place at the same time. This was known as 'the consent principle'.

During the parliamentary debate on the Good Friday Agreement, on 22 April 1998, the MP for Warrington South Ms Helen Southworth recognised the significant step forward into a new future for people in Northern Ireland. She said that people in her constituency had a special relationship with the people in Northern Ireland and had a shared desire for peace. She wanted the House to take a moment to remember Tim Parry and Jonathan Ball – two young boys from her constituency who were killed by an IRA bomb in March 1993. She told the House, 'the terror of that bombing and the shock and pain of those two deaths had a terrible impact on our local community. The families of Tim and Jonathan still live every day with that pain.'[3] Helen Southworth said local people still felt immense grief. She continued:

My constituents know that, for the past thirty years, people in Northern Ireland have faced that terror and pain day after day. More than three-thousand, two hundred people have been killed in those decades. Their families feel the loss, day in and day out. The agreement clearly states, the achievement of a peaceful and just society would be the true memorial to the victims of violence.[4]

Chapter 6

Peace Talks Progress, 1985–98: a Summary

The Anglo-Irish Agreement, 1985

- Britain and the Republic of Ireland signed the deal
- The Anglo-Irish Agreement was signed by Margaret Thatcher and Irish Prime Minister Garret FitzGerald
- It gave Dublin a role in Northern Ireland for the first time in more than sixty years
- Treasury minister Ian Gow resigned in protest and many Ulster Unionists were also against it
- The Ulster Unionist Party (UUP) and Democratic Unionist Party (DUP) led the campaign against the Anglo-Irish Agreement
- The Agreement promoted regular conferences between British and Irish ministers to discuss matters affecting Northern Ireland
- It promised any devolved government would take over from the conferences
- Conference had a consultative role only – with no powers to make decisions or change laws
- For the first time the UK government officially committed to promoting legislation for a united Ireland dependant on a majority being in favour
- The deal was met with anger and bitterness by the majority Loyalist community in Northern Ireland
- MPs at Westminster and the Irish Republic had to agree on all matters

The Downing Street Declaration, December 1993

- This followed talks between the British Prime Minister and the Irish leader

- It said that the people of Northern Ireland should be free to decide their own future
- It called for representatives of various groups to meet and talk
- Sinn Fein was offered a seat provided that IRA violence came to an end
- The IRA declared a ceasefire in August 1994
- A few weeks later there was a ceasefire declaration from Loyalist groups

The Belfast Agreement (or Good Friday Agreement as it would become known), 1998

- It contained proposals for a Northern Ireland assembly with a power-sharing executive
- New cross-border institutions with the Republic of Ireland were promised
- The Republic of Ireland agreed to drop its constitutional claim to the six counties of Northern Ireland
- The Agreement dealt with the decommissioning of paramilitary weapons
- British government commits to reform policing and criminal justice system
- Both governments commit to release prisoners
- Future sovereignty of Northern Ireland, i.e., participation in either UK or Republic of Ireland, to be determined by referendum of people of Northern Ireland
- Right of the people of Northern Ireland to hold Irish or British passports, or both recognised
- Civil rights measures became central to the agreement
- Northern Ireland government to be responsible for: Agriculture and Rural Development, Culture, Arts and Leisure, Education, Enterprise, Trade and Investment, Environment, Finance and Personnel, Health, Social Services and Public Safety, Higher and Further Education, Training and Employment, Regional Development and Social Development

A referendum held in May 1998 showed an overwhelming majority of the people of Ireland supported the Good Friday Agreement. In Northern Ireland 71.2 per cent voted in favour of the Agreement. In Southern Ireland 94.39 per cent voted in favour. In December 1998 Northern Ireland's politicians took their seats at the assembly in Stormont as the Good Friday Agreement came into force. Massive disagreement led to four assembly suspensions and amendments to make it workable in the form of the St Andrew's Agreement in 2006.

Chapter 7

The Bombing of the Grand Hotel

T he Brighton bombing in 1984 was the most audacious terrorist attack ever attempted on the UK government. Certainly it was the most ambitious since the Gunpowder Plot of 1605. Not much has been written about the bomb in any great detail. This is the first book that focuses on the attack in Brighton. Surprisingly, many Thatcherite politicians' memoirs have included very little about the Brighton bombing. The Provisional IRA detonated a bomb at the Grand Hotel in the early hours of the morning of 12 October 1984. Most of the government were staying at the hotel at the time, although Defence Secretary Michael Heseltine and Deputy leader Willie Whitelaw were not at the Grand. The Conservative Party was holding its annual conference in the town.

The Grand Hotel on
Brighton's seafront.
(Photo: Kieran Hughes)

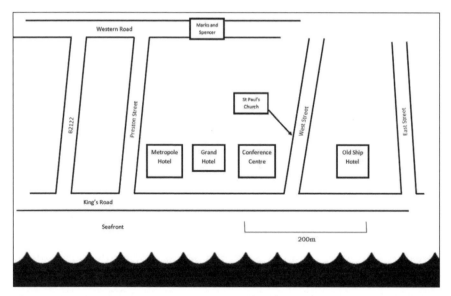

Stategic sites and where they are in relation to the Grand Hotel. *(Image created by Phil Seaman)*

A total of five people were killed in the explosion and more than thirty were injured. It came very close to wiping out most of the government, including the Prime Minister, Margaret Thatcher. Had the attack succeeded, it could have profoundly changed the poltical landscape of the country and affected the immediate future of the United Kingdom. The IRA's Patrick Magee had booked into the Grand Hotel under the false name of Roy Walsh, about a month before. He planted a bomb with a long-delay timer, hidden under the bath tub in one of the rooms (number 629). He was given eight life sentences for the crime, but released from prison in 1999 under the Good Friday Agreement. He served fourteen years behind bars.

It was one of two IRA bombs aimed directly at the collective government of the day. The other was in February 1991 when, at the height of the Gulf War security alert, the IRA fired a mortar bomb directly at Downing Street. The War Cabinet was in session to discuss the threat from Saddam Hussein. The bomb was only yards from hitting the Prime Minister and his senior colleagues. To target the Prime Minister and his War Cabinet on that morning the bomber had to drive into Whitehall, one of the most heavily guarded areas of London, and park in the exact position to take aim. Explosives expert Peter Gurney, who defused some of the unexploded mortar shells in this incident, said the positioning would have to be exact and that they probably used tape on the windscreen and lined it up with nearby buildings. Gurney insists that the measurements were marginally out and that they were very close to getting all three bombs into Downing Street.[1] Patrick Jenkin, later Lord Jenkin of Roding, was Secretary of State for the Environment during the Brighton bombing and had joined the House of Lords four years before the attack on Downing Street. In private correspondence he told me that the mortar attacks on Downing Street in 1991 were 'more of a stunt aimed at proving that elements in the IRA could do such a thing in broad daylight, than a serious attempt to kill people'. He believes that Brighton was a much more serious attack aimed at the heart of government.[2] Other IRA bombings either caused greater loss of life, resulted in more injuries or were of a far greater financial cost. For example, attacks at Omagh in 1998 killed twenty-nine, carried out by the Real IRA splinter group opposed to the Good Friday Agreement, the explosion in the City of London in 1993 cost £1 billion and the Manchester Shopping Centre bomb in 1996 saw 200 people hurt. Devastating as these attacks were, it can be argued that they were aimed at getting attention, disrupting democracy, costing the country money and bullying their way into the political decision-making process. Brighton was more personal and was a direct assassination attempt on Thatcher. It was not a warning, a stunt or a flexing of muscles; this was a direct attempt at killing the Prime Minister and taking as much of the Cabinet as possible with her. In short, the Downing Street bomb was political, Brighton was personal.

Irish Nationalism has been the biggest source of troubles in the UK. As far back as 1761 the Irish Republican Brotherhood and Young Ireland groups were behind the birth of 'Whiteboyism'. Catholics and Protestants were fighting over land in Elizabethan times. Catholics had lands confiscated by Cromwell and Catholics and Protestants fought during and after the Glorious Revolution (1688–1691), when William the Dutch Stadholder was invited over to confront the Catholic King James II. Catholics have experienced 300 years of being sidelined, persecuted or discriminated against. The birth of the Irish Free State in 1922 satisfied some people from a political angle, but the six Irish counties in the North and their attachment to Great Britain created a new wave of troubles. Several wings of Republican fighters emerged or developed over the years, including: different factions of the IRA, the Irish National Liberation Army and the Irish People's Liberation Organisation. Loyalist groups opposed to Home Rule included: the Ulster Volunteer Force, Young Citizen Volunteers and the Ulster Freedom Fighters.

The main theme of this book is to look at the political background, the actual morning the bomb exploded, the rescue attempts and an analysis of how close the IRA came to succeeding in their mission that morning in October 1984. I argue that the bomber made some fundamental planning errors that in reality changed the outcome of that day, and thus the course of history itself. I will also look at security issues surrounding the event and examine the after-effects from several angles. How did it affect Margaret Thatcher? Did it influence the Northern Ireland peace process? I believe it did not have a serious effect on the peace process, evident by the progress made at the Anglo-Irish summit in late 1984 and by the signing of the Good Friday Agreement in 1998. In addition, having spent some time with Patrick Magee and Lord Tebbit, I wish to share my experiences of both interviews. In conclusion, the issue about the lack of writing and research on this subject must be addressed and questioned. In short, what happened, the effects, what went wrong, and why it remains an historical enigma. This is not a study of the IRA, terrorism in general, the Northern Ireland peace process, the Anglo-Irish Agreement or the trial of the bomber, although these issues have to be discussed to put events into context. The book attempts to examine the attack and the political aftermath, among other issues. If there was an abundance of analytical research on the subject, I could afford to concentrate on purely the political effects. However, because this is not the case, I make the deliberate point of focusing on several areas of study.

I first met Brighton bomber Patrick Magee a week before the twenty-fifth anniversary of the explosion, at a pub in central London. I was not sure what to expect and I was worried about whether I should shake the hand of a killer. Magee was polite and helpful and was there to assist me in my undergraduate research into the bombing. I pulled out a list of questions which he looked at and he selected the ones he wanted to answer. We sat quite literally in the middle of the world's busiest and noisiest pub! He declined my suggestion of finding a quiet corner of this large establishment. I think he wanted to be visible and in the open. We talked for about an hour and his comments are analysed later in the

The author Kieran Hughes with the Brighton bomber Patrick Magee in a London pub, 2009. Magee agreed to be interviewed to assist with the author's undergraduate degree research. *(Photo: Kieran Hughes)*

book. As we left I asked a man sitting nearby to take our photograph and he asked us if we were visiting London on our holidays. That photo is reproduced on the opposite page.

Dealing with Terrorism

Governments across the globe have been forced to deal with terrorism for hundreds of years. More recently, the 9/11 attacks in New York, in 2001 (nearly 3,000 killed and thousands more injured), the multiple car bombings in Al-Adnaniyah and Al-Qataniyah in Iraq, in 2007 (hundreds killed) and the sarin nerve-gas attack in Tokyo's subway in 1995 (thousands injured and 13 killed). Russia, Iraq, India, the United Kingdom, United States, Uganda, Iran, Lebanon, Spain, Nigeria – terrorism is global, does not discriminate and is terrifying, sudden and shocking. The various dictionary definitions of terrorism include: 'The use of violence and threats to intimidate or coerce, especially for political purposes.'[3] 'The state of fear and submission produced by terrorism.'[4] 'Threats of violent action for political purposes.'[5] 'The unofficial or unauthorised use of violence and intimidation in the pursuit of political aims.'[6]

The FBI's official website differentiates the definition of terrorism under section 18 U.S.C. 2331 as, terrorism, international terrorism and domestic terrorism. It uses terms such as 'violent acts or acts dangerous to human life that violate federal or state law', 'to intimidate or coerce a civilian population', 'to affect the conduct of a government by mass destruction, assassination, or kidnapping'.[7] Jacob L. Stump and Priya Dixit remind us that terrorism remains a debateable concept with no definitive meaning, citing research that showed more than a hundred different definitions of terrorism when everyday people were asked.[8]

The most shocking terrorist attacks do not always boast the highest fatalities. The Brighton bombing resulted in five deaths. So why is the attack still at the forefront of people's minds? Is it because the terrorists actually got very close to assassinating the Prime Minister? Had they been successful, she would have been only the second serving Prime Minister to have been assassinated. The first was Spencer Perceval in May 1812. He was shot by John Bellingham in the entrance to the House of Commons.

Government response to terrorism at home and abroad has not suppressed the problem or appeased it. One could argue that the aggressive post-9/11 Bush policies antagonised certain sections of terrorists. Indeed, the illegal detention of prisoners at Guantanamo Bay has certainly not helped ease relations with anti-West radicals. Understanding terrorism is key to dealing with it. The IRA did not see themselves as terrorists; the answer is in the title, IRA. They saw themselves as combatants and soldiers fighting a cause. They argued that they were at 'war' with the UK government. This is why they demanded political status at the Maze Prison in Northern Ireland. Sean O'Callaghan, a former IRA member turned informer, stated that the conflict in Northern Ireland was a war in all but name.[9]

At the time of writing my undergraduate dissertation on the Brighton bombing in 2009 and up until writing this book in 2013/14, I have been unable to locate any substantial work purely dedicated to Britain's biggest ever terrorist attack. Therefore, this book aims to look at a number of issues to put this atrocity in its rightful historical place, while linking events to the wider political situation.

Chapter 8

Paramilitary Attacks

IRA attacks pre-dated Bloody Sunday but this list includes some of the worst attacks on mainland Britain since then. Targets were often military, financial or political.

- 1974 – twelve people were killed and fourteen injured after a coach carrying soldiers and their families in northern England was bombed
- October–November 1974 – these weeks witnessed a terrible string of bombs in Britain's pubs. The result was 28 fatalities and 200 people injured
- 1982 – eleven people died and fifty were injured after two IRA bomb attacks on soldiers in London's royal parks
- 1983 – a bomb at Harrods department store in London killed six people
- 1984 – the Brighton bombing – although a smaller fatality rate, the closeness with which this came to wiping out most of the government in one day gave this bombing an alarming political significance
- 1989 – bomb at Royal Marines Music School in Deal, Kent resulted in eleven deaths and twenty-two people injured
- 1990 – two people were wounded following an explosion at an army recruitment centre in Leicester
- 1990 – an explosion at Army Educational Service headquarters in London resulted in seven injuries
- 1990 – a car bomb in Wembley killed one soldier and wounded another
- 1990 – a soldier was shot dead at the train station in Lichfield
- 1991 – a mortar attack on Downing Street came close to killing the Prime Minister and Cabinet colleagues. One of three mortar bombs came within 50ft of its target

- 1992 – three people died after a car bomb exploded outside the Baltic Exchange in London's financial district. Ninety-one people were wounded
- 1993 – two young boys, aged 3 (Jonathan Ball) and 12 (Tim Parry), were killed as a result of bombs in two litter bins in Warrington
- 1993 – the Bishopsgate area of London's financial district was attacked by a truck bomb, resulting in one death and forty-four injuries. The consequence was long-term enhanced security in the area, with roadblocks throughout the Square Mile, later referred to as 'a ring of steel'
- 1994 – IRA ceasefire declared
- 1996 – a large bomb was detonated in the Docklands area of London; two people died in the attack. It caused at least £85 million of damage
- 1996 – the IRA bombed Manchester's Arndale Shopping Centre; 200 people were injured in the blast. It took years to rebuild the city centre afterwards. The explosion mainly damaged the western end of the centre, destroying major chains such as WHSmith, Mothercare, Argos and JD Sports. Parts of the centre were rebuilt and refurbished, at a cost of £400 million

- 2001 – one man was wounded following a car bomb exploding outside the BBC's headquarters in London. This attack was blamed on the Real IRA, according to police reports. The Real IRA is a Republican splinter group that opposes the IRA's ceasefire.

London Docklands area. *(Photo: Kieran Hughes)*

Understanding the Paramilitaries

The struggles in Northern Ireland are a complex set of political and ideological entanglements. This is not a book about the Troubles or the individual groups that have fought on one side or the other, neither is it a book on terrorism. There are plenty of books that go into much greater depth on all these issues. However, this is a good opportunity to look at the simple framework that underpinned the Troubles and paved the way for incidents such as the Brighton bombing.

Feeling runs high in Northern Ireland, based more on national identity than religion. The Catholic and Protestant divide is only an element of the difference. One half want a united Ireland, with the countries in the north joining the south to create the island of Ireland; these are Republicans. The Loyalists want the north to remain part of the United Kingdom. Both sides have political wings. Both sides have paramilitary/terrorist sides.

The main paramilitary group on the Republican side is the Irish Republican Army (IRA) which dates back to the 1916 Easter Uprising. The IRA split into different factions when the 'Old' IRA was accused of failing to protect Catholics under attack from Protestant mobs in the North, and in 1969 the few IRA men who did became the Provisional IRA. The 'Old' IRA became known as the Official IRA. Further splits occurred with the emergence of the Irish National Liberation Army (INLA) in 1974. Meanwhile, the oldest Loyalist paramilitary organisation is called the Ulster Volunteer Force (UVF), established in 1966. This group often responded to IRA attacks with violence again Catholics and Republicans, murdering hundreds of innocent people. In 1972 the Ulster Defence Association (UDA) was created, another Loyalist paramilitary organisation, with violent offshoots labelled as Ulster Freedom Fighters (UFF).

In this book, for simplicity and constraints of space, most references to the IRA refer to Provisionals, certainly those behind the Brighton bombing were Provisionals. The Real IRA, largely ignored in the context of this book, are those IRA members who split from the Provisionals when they declared a ceasefire in 1997. A simple Internet search of Loyalist violence results in 'hundreds' of attacks. A small sample is highlighted here:

1973, February – a Protestant civilian was found fatally stabbed in Belfast. He had also been tortured and burned. It is believed the UDA was responsible for this attack

1976, March – the UDA fatally stabbed a Catholic civilian in Belfast

1979, June – the UDA shot dead an Old IRA member in a shop in Belfast

1981, November – in Dublin, the UFF claimed responsibility for firing shots into the offices of *An Phoblacht*

1988, March – at Milltown Cemetery during the funeral of three IRA members, UDA member Michael Stone attacked the mourners with two handguns and grenades. Three died and more than sixty were wounded

1991, July – the UFF said it planted bombs in eight towns in the Republic or Ireland. Three exploded at a department store in Dublin – others were in shops and pubs elsewhere

1994, January – the UFF claimed responsibility for firing thirty shots at the home of Sinn Fein councillor Alex Maskey.

Chapter 9

The Explosion at the Grand Hotel, Brighton, 1984

In 1979 there was a bombing campaign targeting the British postal system, with six letters defused and nine exploding. The bombs had used circuitry similar to long-delay timers. There was enough forensic evidence to issue an arrest warrant for a man called Patrick Joseph Magee. In 1980 Magee fled to Holland but was arrested. Dutch authorities released him rather than extradicting him to the UK. A few years later he was the man who planted the IRA bomb at the Grand Hotel in Brighton.

It was 15 September 1984 and the Conservative Party Conference was due to take place in a few weeks' time in Brighton. Magee came to bomb the government officials who would be staying at the Grand Hotel, next door to the conference centre. He paid cash for three nights' stay and settled in to Room 629. Magee went unnoticed at the hotel as people went about their business, totally unaware that an IRA bomber was about to set up his deadly work. Magee locked himself in Room 629 and started to assemble his deadly device. He had become an expert in long-delay explosives and he put together his bomb before carefully concealing it under the bath tub. It was 30lb of deadly explosives set up with a long-delay timer. It was carefully wrapped in cellophane as it lay in wait under the plumbing, ready to cause its deadly attack. Magee left the hotel and several guests used that room over the following three weeks totally unaware that there was literally a ticking bomb behind the bath panel, that in theory could have gone off at the wrong time, at any time. The Conservative Party Conference opened on 8 October and the bomb went off in the early hours of 12 October.

The Morning of 12 October 1984, Bomb Explodes: 02.54

Here, I have examined footage of the aftermath of the explosion, interviewed Patrick Magee, Norman Tebbit, police and fire workers and studied reports from Sussex Fire & Rescue. The following pages detail the immediate impact of the explosion and the rescue mission that followed.

The initial call to the East Sussex Fire Brigade was made at 2.54a.m. by automatic dialler. The exact words of the message were 'Explosion at Grand. 300 in building. Call for assistance.' Fire crews first arrived on the scene at 2.58a.m. Later, fifteen fire engines and nine other fire and rescue vehicles were in attendance.[1]

George Hammond was part of one of the first fire and rescue crews at the scene and played a major part in the rescue operation. He discussed his experience with me and said that fire crews on their way to the Grand Hotel that morning all thought that it would be a false alarm. George said

Fireman George Hammond with the author Kieran Hughes. *(Photo: Kieran Hughes)*

they thought 'someone was probably trying to disturb the Government by setting off the alarm – to get them out of bed'.[2]

It was assumed that this was a prank and nobody expected to be greeted with the carnage that they saw. This was no false alarm. The officer in charge of the first attendance was Station Officer Fred Bishop and his first sight of the Grand Hotel revealed that its middle section had collapsed. Bishop knew that fire crews were not supposed to enter a building where a bomb had gone off or if it was suspected that there had been a bomb. He said that he had to make a decision to go in and simply could not afford to waste any time.[3] He could see that floors from the fifth, sixth and seventh levels had collapsed onto the floors below. Rubble, timber and debris were scattered everywhere; carpet, electrical wires, steel, bits of furniture. He was told that there could still be around 250 people inside the building. There was always a chance of another explosion as well. Fireman Ken Towner could not believe the size of the hole in the front of the building. The solidity of the 1860s' construction definitely saved many lives but the explosion still managed to rip through tons of Portland stone and iron from the roof all the way down to just next to the Prime Minister's suite. Very quickly, the hotel was evacuated. Command of the incident was eventually taken over by Chief Officer Eric Whitaker, as reinforcements were called in from nearby fire stations. Very quickly a sea of emergency vehicles was stationed outside the Grand Hotel.

The website fireservice.co.uk states that during the evacuation the fire brigade acquired several master keys to the hotel to check all the rooms. Incredibly they found many people still fast asleep – they had actually slept through a devastating bomb attack and were totally oblivious to the chaos around them.[4] For many, the first they knew of it was when several burly firemen let themselves into their room to get them out of bed. No doubt some women thought they were dreaming! But this was more of a nightmare. The building was unsafe and people were in danger. Rescuers quickly got hotel plans to show who was staying in what room, but as one fireman told me, there were quite a few people in the wrong room in the middle of the night – make of that what you will – but it added an extra complication to the rescue mission.

There were eight main floors of the hotel, and part of the weight of six other damaged floors, collapsed and squashed into the physical space of two floors. Flying masonry had been blown into the street on to cars and promenade shelters. The area in front of the hotel looked like a war zone and the fire alarm could be heard ringing. The walking wounded were soon staggering out into the street and onto the beach with minor injuries and shock. At this point it was obviously a serious situation but noboby knew exactly what had happened. Nobody had declared responsibility.

This was the dilemma facing emergency crews when they got there. The people on the top floor were at the top of the rubble, the people in the middle floors were in the middle of the rubble, and so on. But it was packed tightly together. Fire crews should have been able to work out from the room plans who was where in the rubble. In reality, anyone could have been in this tightly packed section of concrete, masonry and other materials. Although in an interview with the *Daily Mail* in 2014 Lord Tebbit argued the opposite, and said that it had been remarkable how 'nobody seemed to be caught in the wrong bed. Everyone was fully pyjama'd at a Tory Party Conference!'[5]

Assistant Chief Constable David Scott was leading the operation and had been given a list of the 220 guests and 11 staff – although it was estimated that almost a thousand extra guests had attended functions and parties that night. There was no way of knowing who was actually still in the building. Some survivors were

The Grand Hotel after the explosion had ripped through the front section of the building.

Metropole Hotel, King's Road, Brighton. *(Photo: courtesy of Hilton Brighton Metropole)*

already walking away, others had gone to nearby hotels for refuge, such as the Metropole.

The blast had taken out a central chimney stack of the building, causing a massive structural breakdown of a central section of eight floors which partly collapsed into the basement. Fireman said that many lives were undoubtedly saved because the well-constructed Victorian hotel stood strong during the explosion. The collapse only went back one room in depth. The rooms behind those with a sea view were not totally obliterated. Hammond was one of the first firemen on the scene, and one of the most senior fire and rescue personnel on site that morning, helping to lead the operation. I discussed some of the key issues about the rescue, including whether the scale of the atrocities he faced had had a bearing on his view of the IRA, or Northern Ireland politics in general:

No, it didn't change my views on politics, Northern Ireland, or the IRA. I'd been in the brigade twenty years at the time of the bombing. I had dealt with many incidents, and many deaths. To us, that wasn't the government in that building. This really was just another job. Afterwards we became more aware of who it was. After the job we had a de-brief, to ask did we do it right?

Hammond explained that this was not the most shocking incident he had ever been to, and putting it into perspective, explained when he and his colleagues have to attend incidents where children have died it takes the job to a whole new level. He claims Brighton was treated like many others, and it was their task to get the survivors out of the building. He said they would have acted in the same way if it was an explosion at an old people's home or a school.[6] Hammond admitted they started the rescue with four troublesome questions in the back of their minds:

- Is there another bomb?
- Is there a terrorist marksman waiting for us?
- Is it safe to go in, or come out?
- Is the building going to collapse further?'

He explained that because there was no fire, it made the incident slightly easier. He said the brigade may not have been able to pull so many people out of the rubble if there had been flames and smoke and they had been slowed down by cumbersome breathing apparatus. He came to the conclusion that it was this lack of fire and flames that helped in five ways:

- People could walk out of the building
- The damage was less likely to spread
- There were no flames or smoke
- Crews could discard breathing apparatus which would have hampered the rescue
- The chance of all those people being rescued increased[7]

David Hughes from the *Daily Telegraph* recalls:

Fire-fighters were crawling over the building trying to make it safe. A few feeble floodlights illuminated the scene. It looked like a film set. Among the hundreds milling about on the prom, there was a slightly surreal sense of calm. There were no histrionics, no shouting, no flapping. After the alarms were stopped there was almost an eerie silence that did not match the enormity of the situation. People were shocked, but not many appeared to be in shock. It was a very British response to a terrible event. People talked quietly in little huddles.[8]

Other eye witnesses said the same – that once the fire-alarm bells were shut down, there was a strange sense of quiet, as rescuers focused on finding the injured and missing. One major problem was that those early evacuees had left the scene, to find shelter, contact loved ones or to move away from the danger. Therefore, nobody knew who had left and who was still trapped. There were other practical problems that morning as well. In 1984 the fire brigade did not have the equipment that it has today. When they desperatley needed chainsaws to cut through some of the crushed masonry and wood, it was local builders that came forward to donate the saws. In fact, rescuers had to acquire various tools to assist them. Local tradesmen lent petrol driven saws and electrical chainsaws. A building control officer lent a number of Acrow props to rescuers, and a 50-ton crane was supplied from a civil contractor.

A lot of lessons were learned from the Brighton bombing. The fire brigade invested in more equipment, and better equipment, realising it could not rely on begging and borrowing tools from local builders on the next major rescue operation. This became national policy and one of the main operational consequences of the Brighton bombing. It made a big, long-term difference to the fire brigade, not just in Sussex, but in other counties as well.[9] Another dilemma that morning was the fact there was no power. The bomb had knocked out the electricity, and there were no lights in the hotel. The rescue operation was struggling in darkness. BBC TV crews were soon on the scene and lent rescuers their television lights. Without those, the rescue attempts would have taken much longer, and may not have been so successful.

Most of the UK government, including Prime Minister Margaret Thatcher, had been staying at the Grand Hotel that night, although a few members of the Cabinet were not in the building. Willie Whitelaw, the Leader of the House of Lords, was staying at a country estate outside Brighton, and Michael Heseltine, the Defence Secretary, was actually overseas at the time of the blast. Douglas Hurd was staying nearby. In Whitelaw's authorised biography he states that the Attorney General Michael Havers said the Queen would have probably appointed him as a caretaker leader.[10]

Meanwhile, guests and staff had to find a way out of the hotel after the explosion. Detectives had been checking out as best they could a safe route out. They all knew that there was always the chance of a second device going off, carefully timed to catch and kill those fleeing from the first explosion. By 3.05a.m., Mrs Thatcher and her closest colleagues met with Special Branch to plan her escape. It was decided that the Prime Minister had to be taken out of the hotel as quickly as possible to a safe place. At this point they knew it had been a bomb but nobody knew who was hurt or if anyone had been killed. It had become very clear, very early on, that this was an assassination attempt on Margaret Thatcher. Her assistant and friend Mrs Crawford packed the Prime Minister's clothes into a bag and Thatcher made sure her end of conference speech was tucked away safely into her handbag. Then it was time to get out of the hotel. Firemen led the Prime Minister one way, but it was blocked, and they had to turn back. It took several attempts to find a safe way to the doors, avoiding rubble and collapsed floors or blocked doorways. Margaret and Denis Thatcher were hurriedly taken out of the rear of the building under police protection and driven away at high speed to safety. Crawford and the Thatchers were taken to Brighton police station, where the Prime Minister was heavily guarded by armed police. No chances were going to be taken and her personal security officers were on high alert. Later, it was decided that she would get some sleep at the nearby police college and so she was taken out of the front of Brighton police station to a waiting car where reporters were already waiting for her and seeking some answers. John Cole from the BBC wanted to interview her and the Prime Minister was keen to get her message of defiance across, despite the burly and nervous-looking bodyguards trying to hurry her along and keep her moving. This was a very dangerous time and security guards can be seen on footage scanning the people, looking for further threats to the Prime Minister. Thatcher told reporters:

The bomb went off somewhere between quarter to three and three; I know that because I looked up when I had finished something at quarter to three and I just turned to do one final paper, and then, um, it went off. My husband was in bed and all the windows went and the bathroom [in her suite] was extremely badly damaged.[11]

John Cole asked if the conference would go on – Thatcher responded defiantly: 'The conference will go on ... the conference alright, alright John, the conference will go on, as usual'. She was then driven to Lewes Police College under armed guard. Some of her colleagues were flabbergasted that she had insisted that the conference would start on time. However, this was a very 'Thatcher' response to a crisis. It was her way of showing that a terrorist attack would not disrupt the order of the day and that things would continue as normal, without interruption. Some colleagues thought it might have been more respectful to wait for the rescue operation to conclude but Thatcher was determined. However, support came later from an unexpected quarter. Leader of the Opposition Neil Kinnock agreed with the Prime Minister's decision to carry on with the conference uninterrupted, claiming that it was the right kind of decision to make when democracy was under attack.

Thatcher later told a television interviewer that one is usually calm in a crisis when things are happening to you and it is only afterwards that you appreciate the enormity of it all. Thatcher went to church that Sunday and said she was watching the light streaming through the stained glass window and thought to herself that this was the day she was not supposed to see and how grateful she could not see last Sunday what was about to happen. But, she told the interviewer at Thames Television, 'you are dealing with an evil streak in human nature and evil men are just as good at using the latest technology, at thinking it out and placing it'.[12] Thatcher said the bomb had a unifying effect on all democratic people at the expense of isolating the men and women of violence.

In all, the following deaths were reported: Anthony Berry, MP for Enfield Southgate, Roberta Wakeham (wife of Tory Chief Whip John

Wakeham), Muriel Maclean (wife of the leader of the Scottish Tories, Sir Donald Maclean), Jeanne Shattock (wife of the Conservatives' Western Area Chairman) and Eric Taylor, Chairman of the North-West Area Association.

In response, an IRA statement read:

Today we were unlucky, but remember, we have only to be lucky once.

You will have to be lucky always. Give Ireland peace and there will be no more war.[13]

Chapter 10

The Rescue

The Grand Hotel was completed in 1864 with a basement, ground floor and eight upper floors. There were 187 guest bedrooms on the upper floors and staff accomodation too. In May 1972 the hotel made an application for a Fire Certificate. After an inspection was made, a schedule of work was undertaken, although there were some problems because of the complexity of the required works and because it was a listed building. The hotel got its fire certificate in June 1978, along with heat detectors, a new fire alarm and auto-dialler system.

After the alarm was sounded on 12 October 1984, fire engines raced along the Brighton sea front at high speed, dodging fallen masonry and twisted metal. Upon arrival at the Grand Hotel at 2.58a.m., the officer in charge, Fred Bishop, was confronted by 'a chaotic situation'[1] and the most serious blast damage to the building was evident at the fourth and eighth floors. A number of people were already being escorted out by police, through the front and rear of the building. Police were assisting with this evacuation and it was obvious that some people had been injured by flying debris or glass. Despite the chaos there was also a sense of eery calm, with no raging fire or trapped people desperately calling from the balconies. There was just a stream of quiet and calm people spilling out into the street.

One of the first police officers on the scene was Simon Parr. He had already served for thirteen months in Brighton by the time of the explosion. He was a passenger in a police vehicle at the junction of Cannon Place and the seafront, 70yd to the east of the hotel, when the bomb exploded. His first duty was to block the road with his vehicle to stop other traffic from getting through to the hotel. Parr and his colleague assisted people coming out through doors and broken windows. They were all either in evening dress or pyjamas or covered in dust. Parr then went into the hotel to guard the red boxes in the Prime Minister's suite, then held up lighting equipment so people who were trapped in rubble could be rescued by the Fire & Rescue Service. Parr and his other colleagues were by now guarding the inner cordon as the rescue got into full swing. Constable Parr, at the time of writing this account, has risen through the ranks to become Chief Constable of Cambridgeshire. Parr described what he saw when he arrived at the scene, 'massive clouds of dust, screaming, injured people, walking wounded leaving the hotel, gas, alarms, cars, sirens, chaos. Then a strange calmness except for the fire alarm that went on and on.'[2]

At 3.00a.m. Fred Bishop was issuing his first instructions and confirming that there was no sign of a fire after the explosion. There was a considerable amount of dust in the atmosphere that made the search and rescue work more difficult. It was making visibility quite challenging in places. It was some time before this dust settled. The lights at the front of the building had failed as a result of the blast but the lights in the rest of the hotel were still on. The officer in charge carried out an extensive tour of the hotel to further assess the situation and at 3.13a.m. issued further instructions, called for more back-up and indicated that up to 270 people might still be in the building.

A 'major incident' alert was in place just five minutes after the blast. Police moved very quickly and roads within a 3-mile radius of the Grand Hotel were cordoned off in a desperate attempt to slow down or stop the escaping bombers. Police put white tape around the hotel and the conference centre. This was now not just a rescue mission but also a crime scene. As a consequence, twenty of Scotland Yard's anti-terrorist specialists were dispatched to Brighton. Police informed the Royal Sussex County Hospital Accident and Emergency department of what had happened. The duty sister alerted the consultant and shortly after more than 100 doctors, nurses, porters, pharmacists and support staff were on their way to staff the hospital. A separate medical team was dispatched to the Grand. By now there were teams of paramedics, doctors, firemen and police all involved in the rescue mission.

First attandance crews and supporting crews assisted with the evacuation of guests as well as the Prime Minister and senior government figures, who were taken away in police cars. Among the seriously injured rescued during the first stages was Muriel Maclean, who was taken from the sixth floor using a turntable ladder and cage stretcher carrier. By now the Chief Fire Officer, his Deputy and Assistant had been despatched; senior officers Kellett, Hayto and McKinley had all been in attendance since 3.23a.m. Three minutes later the bravery of the fire crews became abundantly clear as they entered the building at the font and rear, heading for the fifth, sixth and seventh floors under the command of Divisional Officer Hayto and up to the fourth floor under the command of Assistant Divisional Officer McKinley. At 3.51a.m. the Deputy Chief Fire Officer wanted to examine plans of the hotel to assist with the search and rescue. There was an additional problem – all of the hotel room numbers had recently been changed, making identification of occupants even more difficult.

By 3.55a.m. there were thirteen fire engines on site, three rescue tenders and one control unit. By 4.00a.m. crews were well underway rescuing trapped people on the ground floor as well as the first, fifth and sixth floors, amid falling masonry and stonework. Several teams were assigned to different parts of the hotel.

Fireservice.co.uk states that 'each person, once found, was given a "Buddy Man" who would talk to the casualty, reassuring him, and explaining what was happening'. This was vital as a way of reassuring those trapped that help was there and to calm them amidst the excessive noise created by the generators and chainsaws being used at the scene.[3] The conference organiser Harvey Thomas was trapped on the fifth floor in a dangerous position, right on the edge of an area that had been completely destroyed. He needed to be rescued as quickly as possible. Between what remained of the fifth and sixth floors Donald Maclean had been located and was trapped in rubble and debris up to his neck, unable to move. Firemen had to be lowered in by rope to rescue him.

By now twenty people had been removed. In 1986, when the jury convicted Patrick Magee of planting the bomb at the Grand Hotel, it heard that bathroom tiles were 'driven like bullets' into Jeanne Shattock's body.[4] She had been in the bathroom of Room 628 at the time of the explosion, very close to the detonation, and stood no chance of surviving the blast. Her husband Gordon Shattock later described his own escape as 'miraculous'. Eric Taylor was in the room below, but did not survive. Gordon fell six floors but was alive.

To reach Harvey Thomas trapped on the fifth floor fire crews entered at this level through the rear fire-exit doors, via an external staircase, at 3.24a.m. They heard cries for help as soon as they got inside. Harvey Thomas was covered in rubble and suspended over what had once been the floor. He had been staying in Room 729 and the bomb had exploded just 7 or 8ft feet below him. It was a miracle that he had survived at all. He was literally hanging over a small section that used to be the floor! There was a collapsed room above him that firemen were trying to secure as well as part of a chimney stack that had survived the blast. The only things holding up Mr Thomas were a door panel, a piece of bed frame and some timber joints, with a drop beneath him of more than 50ft. To make matters worse he was exposed to nearby damaged electrical cables with water pouring down over him from ruptured water tanks. Mr Thomas was not seriously injured but he was in a very dangerous position when he was discovered. The only part of him that was visible was his face. The rest of his body was covered in debris. Despite his big frame – 6ft 4in and 18 stone – he could not move the debris on top of his body. He was also struggling to breath. The committed Christian, whose wife was expecting their child at any moment, was desparate that he would not be taken before his child had seen him. It took eighteen firemen (including back-up crews) and one doctor (Skidmore) to assist with Mr Thomas's slow and careful rescue. The rubble and debris was all moved out of the way bit by bit and Harvey Thomas was eventually slowly pulled out by his armpits. He was finally released from the debris at 5:24a.m.

Dr Skidmore was one of the heroes of the Brighton bombing rescue mission. There were many of course, medical and non-medical. However, this Harley Street doctor was singled out in the Sussex Fire & Rescue report on the incident. Skidmore had been staying at the Old Ship Hotel not far from the Grand itself. Sussex Fire Service said he 'worked unceasingly to comfort those trapped and advised rescuers on how to alleviate suffering. Wherever the rescuing firemen went, Dr Skidmore followed with total disregard for his own safety.'[5] Skidmore was credited with building confidence in casualties and rescuers. The Fire Service claimed that he contributed more to the overall success of the operation than any other individual. When he was woken by the blast, around 300yd away, he put on his jogging gear and ran to the Grand. Police tried to stop him but he announced that he was a surgeon and was let through. He climbed through a broken window and headed to the upper floors, following the sounds of voices calling for help.

One minute after the start of Harvey Thomas's rescue, at 3.25a.m., other crews started to make their way on foot to the sixth floor via an internal staircase. They heard cries coming from the front of the building

The Old Ship Hotel where Dr Skidmore was staying on the night/morning of the explosion and rescue. *(Photo: courtesy of Richard Battrick)*

and needed to know exactly where they were coming from. The picture was becoming clearer – there were lots of people trapped under the rubble and it was a race against time to save them. Donald Maclean was discovered buried up to his neck in debris, situated between a mangled mess of what had been the hotel's fifth and sixth floors. He had been sleeping in Room 629 on the sixth floor when the bomb went off, in the same suite as the bomb in fact. He was pinned down by a large timber joist and was wrapped up in a mixture of floor carpet and bedding. It was near darkness and a very difficult rescue attempt. Mr Maclean was in a precarious position and a fireman had to be lowered 3m down on a line to retrieve to him. The first fireman immediately removed debris from around his head to enable him to breath. Clearing his airways was the immediate priority. They were still working in near darkness until portable lighting arrived at 4.15a.m. which enabled rescuers to work far more quickly and efficiently. It was a painstaking rescue without tools, with a slow removal by hand of small bits of debris. The carpet and sheets were cut away and Mr Maclean was slowly moved onto a stretcher and lowered by a turntable ladder at 4.24a.m. so he could be taken to hospital.

Slightly earlier at 3.45a.m. other rescuers were listening intently to a woman's cry from the mangled entrance foyer. Fire and rescue workers dealing with this section of the building were trying to work out where it was coming from. Rescuers realised that the cries were coming from Lady Berry and they established communication with her. However, she could not be seen under the rubble at all. They realised that she was not seriously hurt, although she was in a distressed state and had been continually calling out and could not understand why nobody had come to her rescue sooner. A fireman had painstakingly and very carefully tunnelled his way through the wreckage to locate her. Rescuers had been encouraged by the fact she was calling out saying she could see their torches. They removed loose timber and rubble piece by piece because any sudden movement could cause further collapse. There were several pauses as it was feared the structure around her was about to give way but it did not and work was resumed. Lady Berry described it as an incredible moment when a fireman eventually got close enough to put his hand on her shoulder.[6] Hydraulic equipment was used to hold up the roof above her head. Ambulance crews had by now been called to the side of the firemen and they managed to feed through an oxygen supply to Lady Berry, as she was finding it hard to breath. By 6.45a.m. the four rescuers involved managed to pull her free from the rubble and she was given medical treatment straightaway.

Still in the dark and with the great danger of further collapse, soon after the discovery of Lady Berry, another team of fire and rescue workers heard voices from about ceiling height on the ground floor. Mr and Mrs Tebbit were trapped about a metre into the wreckage. Rescuers could see three hands poking out of the rubble – that's all. They held their hands and talked to them through the rubble, although they could not see them at all. This practical but kind and supportive gesture enabled rescuers to establish it was the Tebbits and to make sure they were alive. It was also very reassuring for the Tebbits, buried deep inside the rubble. Loose debris was slowly moved away and a mattress was pulled clear. Mrs Tebbit had lost almost all sensation by now and fire crews began to realise how serious her injuries might actually be. After the removal of the mattress, some of Mrs Tebbit's body was visible to rescuers and medical staff who were present. Dr Bellamy was there standing by and was worried that Mrs Tebbit might have broken her neck. Although Mr Tebbit was also trapped in this heap of condensed rubble, they could not start to rescue him as Mrs Tebbit was blocking the way, making her release twice as important so they could get to the next casualty. Throughout the attempt to assist Mrs Tebbit, other firemen were constantly talking to Mr Tebbit to keep him conscious and to reassure him. Only his two hands were visible to them. At 5.44a.m., a support collar was placed around Mrs Tebbit's neck and she was slowly pulled out of the wreckage and put on a stretcher. A total of twelve rescuers and a doctor had been involved in the extraction of Mrs Tebbit. She was then taken to hospital immediately. Steve Tomlin, Alan Farley and Fred Bishop were among the firemen rescuing the Tebbits.

Following the release of his wife, the rescue of Norman Tebbit was underway. He had been asleep in his room when the bomb went off. A horizontal beam was on the small of his back making his removal somewhat difficult for the rescuers. In addition, a large wooden joist was wedging his legs against his chest. Mr Tebbit was in a difficult position. A call went out for heavy duty cutting machinery to saw through the heavy timber joints to try and free him. To get to Mr Tebbit properly a conduit had to be sawn through which meant losing the few lights that they had had access to. That is why the television lights were so intense on Mr Tebbit's removal from the debris because they were the only lights available to rescuers. Norman Tebbit was entwined and trapped by timber, a mattress and various building materials. Rescuers had to coax him out by encouraging him to use his arms as a pivot to free himself from the various obstructions. The mattress was a nuisance and got in the way. His condition was deteriorating quickly and it was a race against time to get him out and on his way to hospital. It took him half an hour to ease himself free enough of the obstructions for rescuers to get in and complete the task. Norman Tebbit was eventually pulled free at 6.53a.m. with Dr Bellamy of the Ambulance Medical Team giving emergency first aid at the scene. Ambulance man Brian Murray took over, giving Mr Tebbit oxygen and dressed his wounds before firefighters carried him to safety. The world was watching as Mr Tebbit, clearly in pain and in distress, was pulled out on a stretcher. He was rushed to hospital by ambulance. Brian Murray's son described his father as a very brave man who did not give a second thought to other possible dangers such as a secondry device going off.[7] The image of Norman Tebbit's rescue as he was pulled out on a stretcher remains the iconic picture of the Brighton bombing.

At 6.30a.m. rescuers established contact with a man calling himself Eric, thought to be Eric Taylor who had been booked into Room 528. As firemen set up a chain of people to remove rubble, others talked to Eric but his conversation faded after about fifteen minutes. Rescuers could not tell where his voice was coming from. They could not get to him quickly enough and sadly Eric did not survive. It was not until 1.30 the following morning, Saturday, 13 October 1984, that Mr Taylor's body was found in the rubble near the ground floor foyer entrance.

After the rescue of Mr Tebbit fire and medical crews continued with their search for other victims. Teams of men kept removing rubble from the ground floor and first-floor levels around the front foyer section. They knew there were still people trapped inside and the rescue mission was far from over. Eventually they found a hand and arm and removed the rubble to discover the body of Sir Anthony Berry who had been booked into Room 328. Dr Skidmore pronounced him dead at the scene.

A line of communication with John Wakeham had been established as Norman Tebbit was being rescued. His very faint moans had been heard by fire crews searching the rubble around the ground floor area. They tried to tunnel towards his voice. It was obvious he was in some real discomfort and fire crews were struggling to pinpoint his exact whereabouts in the heaps of condensed rubble they faced. As rescuers got closer and Wakeham's voice got clearer, his spirits were 'noticeably raised'.[8] He had been sleeping in Room 428 at the time of the explosion. Rescuers were having trouble getting to him from above so a decision was made by senior officers to try and reach him from underneath and rubble was removed from this direction instead. They were faced with the dilemma of a total collapse of the surrounding wreckage above them. The combination of falling condensed masonry, bricks, timber, furniture, pipes and people had not all quite reached the ground. The concertinaed wreckage had to be held up by the Acrow props borrowed from local builders. A collapse could have serious and fatal consequences because rescuers were still not entirely sure what they were dealing with. Firemen kept adding a few more props to try and avoid a total and disasterous collapse. Now chainsaws borrowed from a local plant contractor were used to get through masses of timber and other materials that were still in the way. Eventually Mr Wakeham's head was exposed. More rubble was removed but there was incredible weight bearing down on him from above. Meanwhile, he had lost all feeling in his legs. A large piece of timber against his back was pressing down hard on his shoulder as well. Hydraulic jaws were used to help free him and a team of firemen was assisting and keeping him talking throughout his ordeal. Mr Wakeham had bravely tried to free himself many times but without success. Eventually the assisting doctor gave firemen ten minutes to get him out before he would have to fit an intravenous drip. With a huge effort on Mr Wakeham's part and with considerable help from rescuers, he made one last attempt to pull free of the collapsed rubble. It worked, and he was taken out at 10.16a.m. Wakeham's rescue had become so complex that by the time he was being pulled free about twenty fire and rescue personnel, including the Chief Fire Officer, as well as doctors and other medical staff were all involved in the extrication.

Earlier that morning, at 9.00a.m., an emergency meeting was called to plan where the rescue efforts were to be directed from that point. Those present were: fire and police officers, representatives from the Anti-Terrorist Branch of the Metropolitan Police, Royal Army Ordnance Corps (bomb disposal), hotel management, local authority building control and a civil demolition contractor. The purpose of the meeting was to discuss progress made so far and how the operation should continue. In addition the committee discussed how to identify those still unaccounted for and to get contractors' plant equpiment to assist further with searching the wreckage, despite there being no further communication from anyone trapped in the rubble. Finally, it was decided to scale down fire-brigade operations but at the same time to maintain sufficient personnel to keep the situation operational. By 3.30p.m. the number of casualties who had been taken to hospital was thirty-two, the number of deceased stood at two and there were eight people still unaccounted for.

The brigade scale-down meant having ten fire engines on the scene. Adjacent to where John Wakeham had been trapped rescuers had cut away at carpet and bedding to find the hand of a woman reaching out from under all the debris. There was no pulse and doctors pronounced Roberta Wakeham dead at the scene. There was a sheer drop down into the basement which made the recovery of her body both difficult and dangerous for all involved. The five-man rescue team made sure that props were brought in to hold up the ceiling and hydraulic lifting gear assisted with the removal of Mrs Wakeham's body. At 1.15p.m. she was recovered and removed. She too had been staying in Room 428 at the time of the explosion.

In the middle of the afternoon it was decided that demolition contractors should be brought in to remove excess masonry to stabilise the dangerous structure. Rescue attempts recommenced at 9.17p.m. but only after false reports of a second bomb had come in and been dealt with.

Finally, the body of Eric Taylor was found and removed at 1.30a.m. the following morning. Work continued throughout the night with contractors called in to remove more of the unsafe structure from time to time.

Name of Casualty	Booked into Room No.	Time of Discovery	Time of Removal	Date of Removal	Other Details
J. Taylor	528	3.06a.m.	3.15a.m.	12 October	
G. Shattock	628	3.10a.m.	3.18a.m.	12 October	
M. Maclean	629	3.12a.m.	3.25a.m.	12 October	Hospitalised in critical condition – died
H. Thomas	729	3.30a.m.	5.24a.m.	12 October	
M. Tebbit	228	3.50a.m.	5.44a.m.	12 October	
D. Maclean	629	3.25a.m.	6.01a.m.	12 October	
S. Berry	328	3.45a.m.	6.45a.m.	12 October	
N. Tebbit	228	3.50a.m.	6.53a.m.	12 October	
J. Wakeham	428	7.00a.m.	10.16a.m.	12 October	
A. Berry	328	6.55a.m.	10.45a.m.	12 October	Died
R. Wakeham	428	11.15a.m.	1.15p.m.	12 October	Died
E. Taylor	528	11.38p.m.	1.30 a.m.	13 October	Died
J. Shattock	628	7.40p.m.	11.51p.m.	13 October	Died

Table showing some of the rescued people, their room numbers and time/date of rescue.

Chapter 11

The Conference the Next Morning

Later that morning, the conference continued as Thatcher had insisted on camera to the BBC's reporter John Cole, just hours before. Her private secretary, Robin Butler, who years later as Cabinet secretary played an important part in the Irish peace process, had been working with her just before the bomb exploded. Butler gave Thatcher an urgent message from Michael Heseltine and was sat down as Thatcher read through some papers. It was at this point that the bomb went off and Butler told Thatcher to stay away from the windows, thinking it had been a car bomb outside the hotel. Later that morning, after she had been escorted to safety, Butler was surprised to hear Thatcher declare that they must get to the conference on time. He pointed out that some colleagues were still trapped and others were already dead. Her response was 'we cannot let terrorism obstruct democracy – it's what those people would want. We must start on time.' She called it a British reaction and according to David McKittrick:

> Thatcher radiated defiance and contempt for the IRA in her conference speech, and never lost her strong instinct that the Northern Ireland problem was essentially one of security rather than a political matter. Her attitude to Republicans was that they had to be faced down and defeated. She would say of her decision to go ahead with the conference: 'It was a very British reaction. We were British, that's what it was.'[1]

In a recent interview former government advisor Michael Dobbs told me that Thatcher was deciding the conference should go on even as the masonry was still falling. She was keen that the business of government should continue in defiance, even though many around her were telling her that it should not go ahead.[2] Many were advising her to go to London but she refused. She was determined that terrorism would not be seen as victorious.

After her death in 2013, the *Daily Mirror* discussed Thatcher's decision to open the conference the next morning: 'To many, her defiant reaction – continuing the Tory conference the fatal bomb targeted – was her finest hour. To others, the disaster was part of a war she had escalated against the first and fiercest of her "enemies within".'[3]

In her conference speech that day in October 1984 she received a standing ovation for her comments on terrorism. She spoke without an autocue. Her opening lines were:

The bomb attack on the Grand Hotel early this morning was first and foremost an inhuman, undiscriminating attempt to massacre innocent unsuspecting men and women staying in Brighton for our Conservative Conference. Our first thoughts must at once be for those who died and for those who are now in hospital recovering from their injuries. But the bomb attack clearly signified more than this. It was an attempt not only to disrupt and terminate our conference, it was an attempt to cripple Her Majesty's democratically-elected Government. That is the scale of the outrage in which we have all shared, and the fact that we are gathered here now – shocked, but composed and determined – is a sign not only that this attack has failed, but that all attempts to destroy democracy by terrorism will fail.[4]

At this point many members rose to their feet clapping, to show support. Others were chanting and cheering. Then Thatcher thanked the emergency services that had worked through the night:

I should like to express our deep gratitude to the police, firemen, ambulance men, nurses and doctors, to all the emergency services, and to the staff of the hotel; to our ministerial staff and the Conservative Party staff who stood with us and shared the danger. As Prime Minister and as leader of the Party, I thank them all and send our heartfelt sympathy to all those who have suffered.

Finally, Thatcher's most poignant line in the speech, epitomising her tactics:

And now it must be business as usual.[5]

Thatcher continued by saying, 'We must go on to discuss the things we have talked about during this conference, one or two matters of foreign affairs and after that two subjects I have selected for special consideration: unemployment and the miners' strike. This conference has been superbly chaired – and our Chairman came on this morning with very little sleep and carried on marvellously.'[6] At 3.25p.m. she left to visit the wounded at the Royal Sussex County Hospital. She departed for Chequers at

Defiant Margaret Thatcher.

5.20p.m. Thatcher said in her memoirs, 'I left the hospital overcome by such bravery and suffering. I was driven back to Chequers … faster than I have ever been driven before, with a full motorcycle escort. As I slept that night in what had become my home I could not stop thinking about those unable to return to theirs.'[7] The IRA would have been watching Thatcher make her speech and one wonders whether they felt as if they had failed. Some argue that it brought the Northern Ireland crisis back to the top of the political agenda. If that is the case, then in the eyes of the IRA, the Brighton bombing was a success. To deem whether anything is a success or a failure, one has to examine and understand the objectives.

A few days later on 16 October, the Deputy Prime Minister Lord Whitelaw announced to the House of Lords that:

An evil group has once again planned and carried out an attack on innocent people in pursuit of their aims. They have deliberately struck at the heart of our nation. But they will find that they have simply strengthened the overwhelmingly united resolve of a Government, Parliament and people determined to preserve their free democracy, so long the envy of the world.[8]

Chapter 12

The Aftermath and Reactions to the Bombing

In a letter dated 12 October 1984 the then American President Ronald Reagan wrote to Margaret Thatcher to express his sympathies and support in the aftermath of the attack in Brighton. He said how saddened he was over the fatalities and the injuries sustained by Norman Tebbit and John Wakeham. Reagan offered the expertise of his own specialists to join the team in working to bring the perpetrators to justice. He made reference to the recent summit in London, saying 'terrorist violence is becoming increasingly indiscriminate and brutal, because acts such as the one last night are a growing threat to all democracies. We must work together to thwart this scourge against humanity.' He offered the sympathies of all Americans, referring to the attack as a 'barbarous act'.[1] The letter was followed up with a phone call where Reagan told Thatcher that he deplored this 'horrible attack'.

He said that while a dedicated terrorist 'will always have some success', they must make it as difficult as possible for them. Reagan said that he was especially happy the Prime Minister was not personally injured.[2]

Exactly a month later, in November, the Prime Minister referred to the Brighton attack in her speech at the Lord Mayor's banquet at London's Guildhall. She said whether terrorists pursued their trade in Brighton, Beirut or Belfast they had to be shown that this savagery would only strengthen the resolution of others. To rapturous applause the PM declared that there should be no hiding place or safe haven for terrorists.[3]

At the time of the bombing Thatcher had made her fair share of enemies. The resentment from the hunger strikers lingered on and the miners' strike was constantly on the front pages. When Thatcher passed away in April 2013 there were sickening street parties in some places; ironically held by or attended by people too young to remember her properly. Some of the reaction in 1984 was not much better. Influential singer Morrissey, frontman of The Smiths, said he was sorry Thatcher got out unscathed. The Smiths had started a tour in Northern Ireland that day. David Bret's biography of Morrissey mentions similar remarks and jokes in some of the tabloids in the following days and weeks. He refers to a working-men's club in South Yorkshire that threatened to have a whip-round so the bomber could try again.[4]

In February 1985, Earl De La Warr told the House of Lords that recently the Essex University Students' Union had voted against a motion condemning the Brighton bombing. While young people are often finding their feet politically at this age, many are determined and educated in politics already. Some people were unwilling to condemn the actions of the IRA in Brighton; some even celebrated the attack.

In 1986, English punk band the Angelic Upstarts released a single called 'Brighton Bomb' to celebrate the assassination attempt; an album of the same name followed. The lyrics included the lines, 'the right to take up a fight, and wiped out in a sea of hate, as dust falls in the night. Never to learn till disaster strikes.' The chorus repeated the line 'there's a bomb gone off in Brighton, a bomb gone off to kill'.[5] The Republican newspaper *An Phoblacht Republican News* ran the headline: 'IRA BLITZ BRITS' which echoed an anti-British rule sentiment among some in Northern Ireland. It was an angle of the news that was not heavily publicised back in England. In the days before the Internet such reaction was often kept from the mainstream news.

Some demanded the death penalty for acts such as the Brighton outrage. In December 1985, the MP for Southport, Sir Ian Percival, told the House of Commons that he hoped for support and a sympathetic response to his early day motion 37 on the Brighton outrage, terrorism and capital punishment, claiming 180 honourable members of the House had signed it. He extended the sympathy of the House to the relatives of those killed in the attack, and to those injured as well, describing the incident as:

the indescribably evil and cowardly actions of those who perpetrated this outrage ... death should be the penalty for acts of terrorism causing death ... millions of people regard it as outrageous that anyone should try to kill our Prime Minister and Cabinet – and come so close to succeeding – and, in the process, kill and maim so many ... a debate would give great satisfaction to many supporters of the Government inside and outside the House and to millions of others.[6]

Chapter 13

The Investigation and Trial of the Bomber

Almost immediately Sussex police started to trace every person who had stayed in Room 629 over the previous few weeks. Each occupant was seen, and then eliminated from their inquiries. There was immense pressure to catch the perpetrators and bring them to justice. There was the fear they could try again. Almost 4,000 dustbins and dozens of lorries carrying 46,000 tonnes of evidence was taken away to be sifted through, piece by piece. In there somewhere there could have been vital clues. There was a shortage of bins in the county for months. They had all been bought by those investigating the explosion. Regular people could not buy a bin anywhere.

Detectives stumbled across a problem – they could not trace Roy Walsh. This was because he simply did not exist. During the investigation all the hotel receptionist could remember about Magee – or 'Roy Walsh' as he had called himself, was that he had paid cash in advance for a three-night stay. Miss Trudy Groves allocated him Room 629 as it had a nice sea view, not knowing that it was his intention to blow up the hotel and kill as many people as possible, and hopefully the Prime Minister as well. More accurately, the real Roy Walsh was a known Provisional who was behind bars serving a life sentence at that time.

Meanwhile, the registration card Magee had signed was examined by Scotland Yard. Police used chemicals and laser tests to establish who the prints belonged to. Investigators claimed that Magee's right palm and left little finger prints were exposed on the card. Magee's prints were already on file after he was convicted of three offences as a juvenile. This discovery in Brighton was enough to convict him, although Magee has never accepted that the fingerprint on the card belonged to him. In addition to the prints, further evidence came from the 'Roy Walsh' signature and address. These were given to handwriting experts who decided that they belonged to Magee. The experts picked up on the long base of the figure 2 and the pen not leaving the paper when writing the letter E, with its horizontal strokes. The prints matched those of Patrick Magee who had had his finger prints taken in 1966. Police kept quiet about their main suspect in case he went to ground. He may well have disappeared into a network of IRA safe houses. Six months later Magee returned to Britain and started to put together his next mission. It was at this point that the police and security forces started to track Magee and prepared to bring him in but they had to wait for the right moment.

The Brighton bomb was such an audacious attack that with all the police and intelligence focus it was only a matter of time before they caught someone. The UK government could not be seen to be rolling over and letting anyone get away with an assassination attempt. The success of the police investigation prevented the bombing of other hotels, places in London and seaside towns about to be unleashed by the IRA. Magee checked into the Rubens Hotel on 15 June 1985 and planted another bomb with a long-delay timer. He had checked in under another false name. His room overlooked the Queen's Picture Gallery at Buckingham Palace. As Magee fled to Scotland, detectives were following another suspect who led them to an IRA safe house in Langside Road, Glasgow.

Despite being on a most wanted list, Magee had only been spotted by pure chance while Special Branch was following another IRA suspect who met Magee at Carlisle train station on 22 June 1985. They were tailed back to a Glasgow hideout, at 236 Langside Road. Kevin Toolis, in his article 'Brighton: A Two Way Trial of Bungling and Incompetence', tells how the IRA were unaware of the tail, and an ususpecting team simply opened the door to a team of armed detectives. Inside there were five IRA suspects, including Magee, and more importantly detailed plans of a holiday resort terror wave, with plans to bomb twenty-four south-east England holiday towns.[1] That day all five occupants under surveillance at the Glasgow address were arrested and information at the safe house led detectives to the unexploded bomb at the Rubens Hotel, which was later defused.

The Glasgow safe house.
(Photo: Jim McJannet)

Rubens Hotel, London. *(Photo: Kieran Hughes)*

Reports of a list at the flat at the time suggested a campaign of bombing in the following order: Brighton, Dover, Ramsgate, London, Bournemouth, Rubens Hotel in London, Torquay, Great Yarmouth, Folkstone, Margate, Southend and Southampton.

In September 1986 Patrick Magee was put on trial. The Old Bailey was surrounded by police marksmen as security remained tight for the trial. The jury of six men and six women took five hours, fifteen minutes to reach their verdict on the twenty-fourth day of the trial of Magee. He did not give evidence or call witnesses at the trial. Patrick Magee was given eight life sentences; seven of them were for offences relating to the Brighton bombing on 12 October 1984. The eighth related to a conspiracy to bomb sixteen other targets in London and elsewhere. He was sentenced for planting the bomb, exploding it and on five counts of murder.

However, he insisted at the trial that he was innocent and that the police had made him a scapegoat. He was described by the trial judge as a man of exceptional cruelty and inhumanity. Mr Justice Boreham stated that Magee enjoyed terrorist activities and would serve a minimum of thirty-five years in jail. Four other IRA activists who worked with him were also sentenced at the Old Bailey that day. When he was finally jailed, Magee gave a clenched fist salute as he was led off to start his sentence.

The Old Bailey, London, where Patrick Magee was sentenced. *(Photo: Kieran Hughes)*

Chapter 14

A Study of the Effects of the Bombing on Peace Talks and the Politics of the Day

There are different views on whether or not the bomb in Brighton actually had any real political effect on the Anglo-Irish talks, or the politics of the day in general. McKittrick and McVea state it was the closest the IRA had ever come to striking at the very heart of the British political establishment, and that the shockwaves attacked both Britain and Ireland; but the long, careful, Anglo-Irish negotiations kept creeping forward.[1] However, Caroline Kennedy-Pipe argues that the Brighton bombing stalled the signing of the Anglo-Irish Agreement, and made Thatcher more difficult over negotiations. It is true to say that after Brighton Thatcher said she was 'not going to be bombed to the negotiating table'.[2] Norman Tebbit is adamant that the bomb had NO effect on the peace process in any way, and did not speed up or slow down the talks. He said it made no difference either way and was not a 'turning point', as many have suggested.[3] Patrick Jenkin, now Lord Jenkin, said it was definitely not a critical moment in the Troubles. He claims that the real moment of change was the initiative of the Major government after the first tentative approach by elements in the Republican movement.[4] On the world's political stage Major is indeed widely recognised as doing the hard work on the peace process. Bill Clinton told Lord Stockton at a private party in November 2009, 'the peace process in Northern Ireland would never have stuck without John Major'.[5]

Douglas Hurd was the newly appointed Northern Ireland Secretary at the time, now Lord Hurd of Westwell. In personal correspondence with me over this issue, he insisted 'the Anglo-Irish agreement talks did not stall. With the approval of Cabinet they continued on course.'[6]

Meanwhile, Mary Holland's article 'Ireland Blasts Back' gave a view from the other side of the table. The title of her article alone says it all. She argues there was frustration that the UK government was concentrating on the miners rather than the Northern Ireland issue and that, 'one audaciously placed bomb can do more to concentrate the minds of British politicians on Northern Ireland than endless hours of patient discussion and diplomacy'. She stated, 'their bomb certainly swept away that mood of jaded indifference to the Irish problem'.[7] You cannot blame the security forces for expecting trouble from the miners rather than the IRA. Afterall, the striking miners were the political bone of contention of the day. On 7 June that year, 120 people were arrested during a mass lobby of Parliament by striking miners. On 18 June there were terrible scenes at the Battle of Orgreave when 10,000 striking miners clashed with 5,000 police near Sheffield. This confrontation resulted in dozens of miners and police officers being injured, and more than 90 people being arrested. Police in Brighton were worried there might be a repeat performance outside the Conference Centre or Grand Hotel, in Brighton. However, the counterargument to this is that ten months before the bomb the RUC reported increased activity in Northern Ireland between the IRA and Sinn Fein leaders. In January of 1984 nine high-ranking Provisionals were on the move according to intelligence. They were heading for County Tyrone for what was thought to be an IRA planning meeting upstairs in a pub in Carrickmore, between Omagh and Cookstown. RUC undercover officers were drinking in the bar and monitoring the conversation. The men upstairs were in agreement that Margaret Thatcher was their prime target. They had no idea that they were being listened in on and that the information was being passed on to officials at Downing Street. So Downing Street was expecting an assassination attempt, with information coming directly from sources in the pub where IRA leaders were gathered making plans.

Kevin Toolis, a writer who calls Thatcher 'Maggie the Monarch' and sarcastically 'The Real Queen of England', says that in the weeks after Brighton a small group of Conservative and Unionist MPs were trying to ruin the talks to stop any notion of joint sovereignty of Northern Ireland between Southern Ireland and Britain. Indeed, press conferences with Hurd and Thatcher in November 1984 had a tone of 'limited' or 'no' chance of joint sovereignty.[8] Douglas Hurd's biographer Mark Stuart says the talks were bumpy after Brighton and that Geoffrey Howe and Ireland's Prime Minister Garret FitzGerald were desperately trying to get Thatcher to focus on compromise to combat terrorism. Brighton had hardened Thatcher on the issue.[9] But the argument over whether Brighton swayed or delayed the talks in any way is subjective. For example, the former Northern Ireland Secretary James Prior had already publicly taken a hard Unionist stance three months BEFORE Brighton. Four months before the IRA bombing of the Grand Hotel the Prime Minister had authorised the secret negotiations with the Republic of Ireland but it was almost abandoned after the attack. Downing Street aide Charles Powell said Thatcher had warned 'the bomb has slowed things down and may in the end kill any new initiative'.[10] However, the bomb did not slow matters down, the Anglo-Irish Agreement was still signed and efforts were made to bring about peace.

In the weeks and months before the Good Friday Agreement came into force, in 1998, opposition to its principles was still public and very vocal. The success of the Anglo-Irish Agreement was down to the principle of consent, and the triple lock of parties, parliament and the people. Therefore, all-round support was crucial in making it work. It was the same in 1998.

The Revd Ian Paisley, unsurprisingly, made a passionate parliamentary speech about the proposed release of all prisoners, no matter how murderous. Paisley wanted to mention some of the people being proposed for release, to make his point more clearly. He acknowledged that Republicans say there is no justice in the courts of Northern Ireland and no juries, so do not recognise the sentences. So he wanted to use two examples that had been through the British justice system.

He started with Patrick Magee, who he reminded was behind the audacious attack in Brighton, aimed at Prime Minister Margaret Thatcher but killing five others instead and injuring many more. The man of 'exceptional cruelty and inhumanity' (the trial judge's description) would be out walking the streets a free man as part of the Agreement, Paisley pointed out. He then turned his attention to Paul Kavanagh, an IRA member who took part in the month-long London bomb campaign in 1981, including attacks on Chelsea Barracks. Despite a sentence of thirty-five years and the likelihood that no Home Secretary would ever release him (the trial judge's warning), he too would be walking the streets a free man under the Agreement warned Paisley. He also pointed out that there were outrages on both sides and that Johnny Adair (Commander of the Ulster Freedom Fighters) would also be out, a free man within a few years. Adair (the trial judge condemned him as being dedicated to the cause of naked sectarianism) was believed to have organised the shooting of up to twenty people, and was jailed in 1995.

The Northern Ireland (Election) Bill had its second parliamentary reading on 22 April 1998 with the Revd Ian Paisley attacking some of its supporters who said repentance from IRA activists in jail should be taken into account when considering the early release part of the Agreement. Paisley said:

The Hon. Gentleman knows little about what is happening in the gaols of Northern Ireland. I know plenty, as I have been a prison chaplain for years. There is no sign of repentance in the gaols. They are run as academies for terrorism. The slogans are on the wall. When a person is killed outside, the cheers go up in the prisons. I have heard them.[11]

Paisley acknowledged that people on both sides of the religious divide had lost loved ones and said victims' families often asked him, 'What did they die for? To have the killers let out because an agreement has been made?'[12] Paisley denied that the Agreement was a way forward to peace because Republicans negotiated while the IRA still had weapons, so it was not a level playing field. He said, 'The people who have put their finger on the

Agreement have not apologised by any act or word.'[13] However, despite Paisley's concerns, many politicians from all sides were firmly in favour of the Agreement.

On 26 November 1986 Margaret Thatcher announced to the House of Commons that 'this House approves the Anglo-Irish Agreement signed on 15th November by the Prime Minister and the Taoiseach [Irish Prime Minister], Dr Garret FitzGerald. Since 1969, nearly 2,500 people have lost their lives in Northern Ireland as a result of terrorism.'[14] She acknowledged the historic divisions between the two communities in Northern Ireland, which she said could not be ignored. Thatcher recognised the need for deep sympathy for the thousands of families whose lives had been affected by the gunman and the bomber. She said that any initiative to bring the people of Northern Ireland closer together to beat the terrorists created fears from past events but she said she did not believe them to be justified.

Ken Maginnis, MP for Fermanagh and South Tyrone, said to the House:

> I do not believe that the Anglo-Irish treaty is only worthy of criticism because it is a bad agreement. It is an evil thing conceived from a clandestine relationship, in which there is an element of deceit ... the Anglo-Irish agreement was devised without any input from the seventy per cent of the Ulster population who wish to remain within the Union ... I have watched the Secretary of State for Northern Ireland's pathetic efforts to justify this agreement during the past ten days.[15]

Chapter 15

The Post-bombing Cabinet Meeting

Meanwhile, back in 1984, the first Cabinet meeting after the Brighton bombing took place in Downing Street, on Thursday 18 October 1984, at 11 o'clock in the morning. Records from The National Archives, released on 3 January 2014, show that the meeting was not at all dominated by talks about Brighton and that the machinery of government was evidently still turning. This particular Cabinet meeting discussed issues relating to South Africa, Iran/Iraq problems, coal pit attendance, the fact that British industry only held supplies of coal to last a further four weeks, as well as a reflection on the Prime Minister's recent talks with the President-designate of the European Commission, Monsieur Delors.[1] In fact, the talks had taken place in between the Brighton bombing and this Cabinet meeting; further evidence that it was business as usual. Cabinet minutes refer to talks taking place between 15 and 16 October. However, Margaret Thatcher did start the Cabinet meeting on this day by expressing deep sympathy for the bereaved and the injured from the previous Friday. Her thoughts were especially with Norman and Margaret Tebbit who had suffered serious injuries.

Deputy Prime Minister Willie Whitelaw said that he had already discussed security issues with the authorities at the House of Lords after the bombing and had called for stricter security measures, including staff name badges and spot-checks. John Biffen, the Lord Privy Seal, called for speedy action and a swift solution to the issues over divided responsibilities between the different sides of Parliament. The House of Commons's authorities, he assured Cabinet, were putting together a list of measures to be considered by the Joint Committee on Security. The Prime Minister concluded the meeting by reiterating the importance of urgent and effective precautions.

Five weeks after Brighton the effect that the explosion had had on Margaret Thatcher was apparent. At an Anglo-Irish Summit at Chequers the bombing had no doubt had time to sink in, and the exact details of all casualties and fatalities were then known. At this summit Thatcher was throwing out suggestion after suggestion, saying 'this is out' and 'that is out'. Her speech at the summit was dubbed the 'out, out, out' speech. One could argue that the Anglo-Irish peace talks were in crisis, almost definitely because of the effects of the Brighton bombing, and almost definitely because of Thatcher's reaction to the whole incident and what it meant politically and personally. She certainly did not want to come across as weak. Looking at the bigger picture, the talks had been going on since 1980. Kennedy-Pipe argues American influence over Northern Ireland, Thatcher's understanding of American depth of feeling, and the President's plea for progress allowed for the Anglo-Irish Agreement to be signed the following year.[2] One could therefore argue, that the Brighton bomb put back the talks by many months, but 'not' many years. However, many point out that the bombing was very significant in the long-term. The *Daily Mirror* said of Thatcher's response, 'It also stiffened her resolve and when talks resumed she was intransigent, despite increased US pressure.'[3]

Henry Patterson argues that Brighton made Thatcher reluctant to innovate when it came to peace talks.[4] He agrees with Kennedy-Pipe that it was only her desire for good relations with the United States that kickstarted progress again. The bombing derailed everything according to Ros Wynne Jones's 2013 article 'After Thatcher's Death'.[5]

Back in 1985, even the Cabinet was split on which way to go. Thatcher, Foreign Secretary Geoffrey Howe and Cabinet Secretary Sir Robert Armstrong favoured a radical plan that would undermine the Irish Republicans. Howe does not attach any delay or negative effects of the bombing to the Anglo-Irish Agreement, stating he was relieved the bombing did not stop the talks and only made the Prime Minister stronger over security co-operation with Ireland, but that it reinforced the dominant importance of closer security.[6]

Downing Street correspondence to Cabinet Secretary Sir Robert Armstrong from Charles Powell, Margaret Thatcher's private secretary, indicates political caution after the Brighton bombing, and not a collapse of talks. Political commentators like to analyse whether the bombing de-railed the peace talks. It was quite reasonable to handle them differently after such a significant event.

There is evidence from Downing Street letters made public in January 2014 that Thatcher tried to cool negotiations after Brighton. Some of her language to advisors was negative, expressing concern that the bomb had slowed down talks and might finish them altogether. The Prime Minister said talks should indeed go slowly or perhaps stop. Charles Powell subsequently wrote to Sir Robert Armstrong saying that the Prime Minister did not want him (Armstrong) to discuss a possible communiqué for the Anglo-Irish Summit with Irish officials. This was evidence that Brighton slowed talks. However, a number of low-key meetings did occur to discuss Anglo-Irish matters. They took place *after* Brighton and were known as the 'Armstrong/Nally talks' (15–16 October) after Sir Robert Armstrong and Dermot Nally, the then secretary to the Irish government. These talks led up to the summit at the end of 1984 and were also the foundations of the Anglo-Irish Agreement a year later, in November 1985. Therefore, work on Northern Ireland, including discussion on devolved government, took places in the days, weeks and months following the Brighton bombing. This goes against the popular headline about how Brighton de-railed talks. The evidence shows that there was a lot of work going on in the background to help address the Troubles. Further evidence that Brighton did not de-rail peace talks comes in the form of a letter to Charles Powell from the Northern Ireland Office in Whitehall. The letter said that Douglas Hurd planned to meet the Northern Ireland party leaders for discussions on political development in the week commencing 5 November, sometime before the November summit at Chequers. Hurd's talks would be based on James Prior's speech to the House of Commons on 2 July of that year. This shows a co-operative continuity from July, through the bombing and out the other end for the Armstrong/Nally talks, Hurd's discussions and the November summit.

The letter dated 15 October, just days after the bombing, said 'the events last Thursday night in Brighton have confirmed the Prime Minister in her view that we must go very slow on these talks and must at all costs avoid the impression of being bombed into making concessions to the Republic'.[7] It goes on to say that the PM still favoured exploratory talks, although there were some provisos – again, this demonstrates caution and the letter stated how the PM needed time for reflection over certain matters. This shows that the bombing did NOT derail talks. In fact, Dr Clive Walker writes that the bombing may well have 'encouraged' the Anglo-Irish Agreement in 1985.

It is well known that straight after Brighton there was a serious government split. Chris Patten and Michael Mates wanted to talk further to Dublin and get closer co-operation with the Irish government. However, Thatcher was rather less keen to have Dublin at the table post-Brighton, in case it was seen as giving in to the IRA. At this point Holland argues: 'If, it now seems possible the Government is going into a state of funk about the fragile consensus which is seemed to have reached with Dublin, then the bomb which blasted the Grand Hotel in Brighton will have succeeded beyond the IRA's wildest dreams.'[8]

By July 1984 the Northern Ireland Secretary James Prior said none of the options in the report were workable. However, by September, he had been replaced by Douglas Hurd. By now peace talks were stalling. This was just immediately before the impact of the Brighton bombing. Was this lack of progress instrumental in forcing the IRA to take drastic action? On 13 October 1984 Douglas Hurd delivered a speech to the Conservative Party Annual Conference, rejecting the three main options that had been proposed in the New Ireland Forum Report. Although the Northern Ireland debate was already on the programme for this day, before the bombing, it is unclear historically whether his speech was altered to send a message to the IRA, although at this point Hurd was careful not to blame them for the atrocity. In my private correspondence with Hurd, I addressed this issue and he told me 'No, my speech at the Conference was only slightly re-worded to take account of the bomb and our reaction to it.'[9]

Interestingly, three days later Thatcher said that she was not in favour of any 'sudden new initiative' on Northern Ireland. Again, it is impossible to ascertain whether or not these comments were altered because of the bombing. On the 19 November 1984 Garret FitzGerald, then the Irish Prime Minister, met Thatcher at Chequers for the Anglo-Irish Summit.

Former Tory MEP Lord Stockton, grandson of former Tory Prime Minister Harold Macmillan, has his own views on the link between the bombing and the Anglo-Irish agreement. He is a close friend of Lord Tebbit, and had worked with Margaret Thatcher on many occasions. Stockton left Room 331 at the Grand Hotel after drinks with Lord McAlpine, about an hour before the explosion. He told me that the Anglo-Irish Agreement talks stalled because the attack gave new energy to Unionists and people like Ian Paisley who put pressure on the government not to talk to 'terrorists'. But Stockton said Thatcher went through the motions anyway and signed the Agreement as she would have done even if there had been no bomb, but as he puts it, it was just a symbolic signing and several agreements had been signed before, and since. It was former Prime Minister John Major who did the real work in pushing the Agreement forward and getting it to the weapons decommissioning stage, during his time in office. Stockton believes this progress would have happened anyway, and the bombing may have delayed progress, but only temporarily. Therefore, it seems as though there was more turmoil post-Brighton, but talks continued at a slower pace, with sterner faces, but with the end result probably being the same.

Here, one can see how years and years of work, from talking, to the signing, to decommissioning, to voting for the Assembly almost puts the Brighton bombing in the shade. The hard work behind the scenes went on regardless. Stockton believes this process would have continued with or without the attack on the Grand Hotel in 1984.[10] Richard English, Professor of Politics at Queen's University, Belfast said, 'The real significance of the bombing lies not in its impact on the emergence of a peace process, but rather in its demonstration of the lethal capacity of the IRA to produce devastating political violence, and in the awful suffering that was inflicted on the actual victims of the bomb.'[11]

It is not just the Anglo-Irish Agreement that arguably stalled, or was shaken, as a result of the Brighton bombing. The terrorist attack had other effects on Thatcher and the government. Lord McAlpine (in Room 331 at the time of the blast), said that the shock of the explosion, although having killed a small number of people, had had a profound effect.[12] In 2004 a Channel Four documentary highlighted crisis after crisis post-Brighton; policies were shelved and U-turns made. Thatcher herself admitted that things were derailed in the immediate aftermath of the bombing, partly because some of her key supporters, like Tebbit and Wakeham, were still not at work. It is clear, the terrorist attack had badly shaken the government. Most of them had come relatively close to being killed. Thatcher insists the following few months were very difficult:

It became a time when we stumbled over small things, and were stopped from doing some of the things I wanted to do because you just couldn't go ahead, the timing just wasn't right. For example, this was the period we came into Westland. This was the period when we wanted to privatise British Leyland and we were stopped from doing that.[13]

Despite the enormity of the blast, it was the government's ambition to function as normally as possible. The first step, of course, was to carry on with the conference. Thatcher resisted all police demands to be rushed back to Downing Street. Instead, she announced the conference was still on. Norman Tebbit, Secretary for Trade and Industry, had an office installed in the hospital where he was being treated, first in Brighton, later at Stoke Mandeville. In his memoirs he states 'even on that first day the machinery of Government was able to react'.[14] Government whips also organised themselves, and Mr Tebbit was supplied with his own phone next to his bed to liaise with his number two, Paul Channon. Norman Tebbit recalls the constant stream of private secretaries and civil servants visiting him and his wife in hospital, and how they became friends of them both. He recalled, 'I doubt if many other Private Secretaries have helped their Minister put on his shoes and socks, fed his wife and read poetry to her late at night.'[15] From Stoke Mandeville Tebbit worked on the £4 billion privatisation of British Telecom. The decision on pricing and the allocation of shares was taken from hospital.

In private correspondance Douglas Hurd told me he recalled 'no immediate effect of the bomb blast on the political machinery of the day'.[16] This is clearly a matter of opinion, rather than a matter of history. Some politicians thought they had been affected in their work by the explosion and the aftermath, Thatcher, for example. Others, such as Hurd and Tebbit, either refused to acknowledge it, or truly believed that it really was business as usual. It can be argued that whatever the effect on the

The entrance to Stoke Mandeville Hospital. *(Photo: Kieran Hughes)*

machinery of government, if any, a brave face was put on by all. Margaret Thatcher was seen by her political allies as a great hunter. She liked to take on the big enemies, and the big problems, and win. She took on the unions, and won. she faced up to Argentina's General Galtieri, and won. She took on the hunger strikers, and won. She took on the miners, and won. Here, at Brighton, the tables were almost turned, the hunter became the hunted. I would argue anti-British feeling among Republicans was running at an all time high in the early 1980s. The funeral of hunger striker Bobby Sands was attended by 100,000 people. He had become an iconic image in the graffiti of the Nationalist areas. Thatcher, in the view of his supporters, let him starve to death. She took a hard line, reminding people that it was his choice, he was a criminal and he chose to die.

As far as we know, the IRA had never before considered a serious attempt on the life of a British Prime Minister, probably due to the fact that such an attempt, even if successful, would be counterproductive, galvanising popular support for the UK government, and creating a back lash of crackdowns and punishments. In this case, however, the IRA leadership decided that Thatcher simply had to be killed, along with as many of the Cabinet as possible. G. Davidson Smith says the IRA traditionally carried out the biggest attacks prior to their annual meeting which took place weeks before, in Dublin. On this account, security services should have been expecting something.[17]

Chapter 16

The Wheels of Government
Kept Turning Around

The determination that the everyday business of government should carry on and not be affected by a terrorist attack was echoed in both Houses of Parliament in the days following the blast. In the House of Lords on 16 October 1984, Lord Cledwyn of Penrhos declared his determination that attacks like this should not affect how the government goes about its business, announcing that 'after security is tightened and necessary additional precautions are taken, we must not allow this act of barbarism to interfere with our democratic duties, responsibilities and liberties in a free society'.[1] Baroness Seear, leader of the Liberals in the Lords, echoed the sentiment by announcing to the Lords:

> May I also say how heartily we agree that, horrible though this occurrence has been, it should not be allowed in any way to interfere with the way in which we conduct our political affairs in this country. If politics has become more dangerous, we must, of course, take all the sensible steps that we can to make it safer but not allow ourselves to be diverted from our main purpose.[2]

Meanwhile, one of the impacts of the Brighton bombing was unification argued Thatcher – she claimed it brought people together and intensified their anger towards the IRA. The Deputy Prime Minister made comments along these lines in the House of Lords on 16 October 1984, saying 'they [the IRA] have simply strengthened the overwhelmingly united resolve of a Government, Parliament and people determined to preserve their free democracy'.[3] The Prime Minister often said publicly that it had a unifying effect on all democratic people in isolating the men and women of violence. In truth, however, what the bomb did was magnify sentiment on both sides. Those on one side of the political divide felt a sense of achievement and camaraderie in what had happened. On the other side, they felt defiant and stood proud in the face of terrorism. There was also a similar effect in government. They pulled together to keep things moving. The key to the perception that government had won and the IRA had lost, it can be argued, was the public demonstration that it was business as usual in Whitehall. The Prime Minister knew this; she was experienced at dealing with terrorist attacks. Within hours, government was indeed fully operational. The government had to keep running as best as possible to combat terrorism. It would have been easy to take a few days off, especially to allow police to carry out their investigation. But Thatcher was determined that the bomb would not stop the conference. She said in her memoirs that she was advised to go back to Downing Street immediately but she refused. In her memoirs she recalls:

> There was discussion about whether I should return to No. 10; but I said, no: I am staying. It was eventually decided that I would spend the rest of the night at Lewes Police College. I knew that I could not afford to let my emotions get control of me. I had to be mentally and physically fit for the day ahead ... all of us were relieved to be alive, saddened by the tragedy and determined to show the terrorists that they could not break our spirit.[4]

Lord McAlpine called the Chairman of Marks & Spencer to arrange for it to open very early, later that morning. Many of those due at conference had lost their clothes in the blast. They were all kitted out at M&S the following morning. At 9.30a.m., as promised, the conference started, almost as if nothing had happened, everyone looking smart!

Lord McAlpine had made the arrangements by contacting the security officer at Marks & Spencer's headquarters in London. The bill for the extra clothing came to £6,000. It was a bill that had to be authorised as there were many party members who had lost their clothes, some taking refuge at the nearby Metropole, wearing pyjamas and nightdresses. Once everyone had been dressed appropriately, the conference went on as planned, as instructed by the Prime Minister. Margaret Thatcher took to the stage and, supporters would argue, delivered one of her most powerful speeches ever, without a script or an autocue. She was drowned out by applause and chanting.

She paid tribute to the dead and injured, and thanked the emergency services and hotel staff. Then, it could be argued, her crucial underlying message to terrorists, was her message to conference, 'and now it must be business as usual'.[5] After the conference Margaret and Denis Thatcher visited the injured at the Royal Sussex County Hospital.

Some hold a strong view that Brighton did indeed have a detrimental effect on both Thatcher and the political machinery of the day. Lord

Royal Sussex Hospital, Brighton. *(Photo: reproduced by kind permission of the Brighton and Sussex University Hospitals NHS Trust)*

Stockton claims 'what scared her [Thatcher] the most was the – we only have to be lucky once – warning. I think she rushed things through after that, thinking if she may be killed, she couldn't afford to waste time, and a perfect example of this was the poll-tax fiasco.' Stockton argues the biggest by-product of the Brighton bombing was Margaret Thatcher now thinking she was vulnerable.[6] But Lord Jenkin, although acknowledging how shaken she was at the time, believes her decision to hold the conference the following day as planned showed her determination, and showed her character as a 'major, natural leader'.[7] Eight months after the bombing *TV-AM*'s David Frost asked the Prime Minister if it was true, as a lot of her friends claimed, that personally she had been greatly affected in her priorities, beyond the political issues, by the tragedy that happened at Brighton. Frost asked if she could sense a change in herself? Thatcher avoided the real answer and talked about how events like Brighton made you put things into perspective and how important health, strength and friends are.[8] Norman Tebbit was interviewed by the *Guardian* newspaper after her death and said 'I think she always felt bad about Brighton because clearly the intention was to murder her, but she walked away and a number of her friends died instead. She didn't talk about it. We didn't talk about the impact it had on my life. I suspect in many ways we were alike in that way'. Tebbit discussed the similarities between the two of them, a spirit of getting up and getting on with it, without complaining.[9]

Meanwhile, Laurent Murawiec wrote an article on 6 November 1984, called, 'After the Brighton bombing: Who will end Britain's political paralysis?'. Murawiec claimed he could see an instant effect on the government of the day, stating, 'a degree of confusion is apparent in the day-to-day situation, with the government showing an increasing loss of grip in the face of domestic and international events'.[10] This was a sweeping analysis because how many crucial events really took place between 12 October and 6 November 1984? Murawiec goes into great detail about the miners' strike after this statement but the strike was already underway before the Brighton bombing. What Murawiec fails to acknowledge is the conference starting the following day on time, Tebbit orchestrating the privatisation of British Telecom from his hospital bed at Stoke Mandeville in Buckinghamshire, support for the Conservative government improving after several months of poor poll showings, with the latest MORI poll putting them nine points ahead of Labour on 44 per cent, and 800 miners ending their strike and returning to work on 5 November 1984. This is not the evidence that backs up the sweeping anti-Tory statement by Murawiec.

Thatcher was politically thick-skinned, but comments from people like Seán MacManus must have had some effect on her. After the Brighton bomb, the Sinn Fein politician publicly announced, 'I was heartbroken when Thatcher wasn't killed in the Brighton bomb. I would have no moral crisis over that at all. Of all the people representing the British Establishment she had no redeeming aspect or facet. During the hunger strike, she played games with people's lives. There was no human side. Also, the way she treated the miners. Bringing her into society was a waste of time.'[11] Republican journalists like Mick Hume were quick to highlight animosity to Thatcher in Britain itself, pointing out what an ex-miner told him in Pontefract. 'See what those Irish bastards did? They ***ing missed her!' Hume claims people supported the bombing, not because they backed Republican ideologies, but because they just hated Thatcher and her treatment of the miners.[12]

Chapter 17

How Close Did the IRA Really Come to Killing Margaret Thatcher?

P atrick Magee very nearly succeeded in assassinating the British Prime Minister. Had he accomplished his mission, it would have been only the second time in British history that a serving prime minster would have been assassinated. He may have been disappointed that he did not get Thatcher but the signing of the Anglo-Irish Agreement a year later was seen by some as Thatcher's weakening over Northern Ireland.

The bomb had gone off on the sixth floor, which came crashing down in a vertical line killing Muriel Maclean at the top, then Jean Shattock, before descending and killing in its path Eric Taylor, Roberta Wakeham and Sir Anthony Berry. It stopped short of the next level where it may well have taken out Sir Geoffrey Howe and his wife. By this calculation, it may not have been the positioning of the bomb that caused it to miss its main target but perhaps too few pounds of explosives. A few more may well have powered the explosion another few fatal feet; just one more floor and either side as well. At a simple level, Mrs Thatcher was simply in the right place at the right time as well. David Moller pointed out that had she not been in the sitting room at the time of the explosion studying an urgent last-minute document given to her by private secretary Robin Butler, she would have been in the bathroom preparing for bed. Moller states 'the blizzard of flying bricks and glass would have almost certainly killed her'.[1]

In her memoirs, Margaret Thatcher said that 'those who had sought to kill me had placed the bomb in the wrong place'.[2] The IRA had indeed got the wrong place, but only just. It is widely accepted that the terrorists had

Room numbers and occupants

Floor	...23	...24	...25	...26	...27	...28	...29	...30
8th				Staff				
7th				Staff	726 Rt. Hon. & Mrs. N. Soames	727 Rt. Hon. & Mrs. N. Lawson	728 Sir Walter & Lady Clegg	729 Mr. H. Thomas
7th (cont.)								730 Mr. and Mrs. G. Younger
6th	623 Mr. Harris	624 Mrs. Hamilton	625 Sir Keith Joseph	626 Mr. & Mrs. Wyldbore Smith	627 Mr. & Mrs. Price	628 Mr. & Mrs. G. Shattock	629 Mr. & Mrs. D. McClean *	630 Mr. H.E.A. Parsons
5th	523 Baroness Airey	524 Mr. I. McCrone	525 J.M. Dalgleish	526 Mr. A. Thomas	527	528 Mr. & Mrs. E.G. Taylor	529 Mrs. E. De La Motte	530 Mr. and Mrs. J.V. Elwes
4th	423 P.J. Cropper	424 Sir Anthony Carmer	425 Mr. Henderson	426 Mr. & Mrs. C.J. Curry	427 Mr. & Mrs. W.D. Morton	428 Mr. & Mrs. J. Wakeham	429 Mr. & Mrs. S. Odell	430 Mr. & Mrs. Fry
3rd	323	324 Mrs. J. Burnham	325 Mr Billings	326 Sir Ian & Lady McLeod	327 Mr. & Mrs. Lawrence	328 Sir Anthony & Lady Berry	329 Lord & Lady Denman	330 Sir Basil & Lady Feldman
2nd	223 S. Prendergast	224 Lord Belstead	225 Sir Ronald Millar	226 Mr. & Mrs. B.E. Rhodes	227 Mr. & Mrs. Barnard	228 Rt. Hon. & Mrs. N. Tebbit	229	230 Rt. Hon. & Mrs. J.S. Gummer
1st	123 Mr. I. Lang	124 E. Nicholson	125 Sir James Goold	126 Rt. Hon. & Mrs. L. Brittan	127 Sir Geoffrey & Lady Howe; Eugene Suite	128	129 Napoleon Suite	130 Rt. Hon. M. Thatcher & Mr. D. Thatcher

Additional 3rd floor: 331 Lord & Lady McAlpine

Additional 2nd floor: Manager's private flat (230)

Additional 1st floor: 331 / 135 Sir Russell & Lady Sanderson; 134; 131 Private Secretary

Ground: Dining Room | Entrance | Kitchens | Lounge Bar

Basement

The explosion went off where it is marked with an asterisk, in Room 629, with the force directed towards Room 628.

wanted to put a bomb in, or near, Thatcher's room. Here, my new theory shows the IRA got the right room, but the wrong side and was just a few feet away from achieving what they wanted. First, one needs to study the layout of the rooms, then it is vital to look at who was staying where when the bomb went off, and which rooms collapsed. A central part of the structure, near the front, but excluding the 'whole' of the front wall, went down.

The bomb was planted behind the bath panel in Room 629, up against the right side wall as you look at the hotel. It was on a long-range timer set to go off weeks ahead. This type of planning, according to Peter Chalk, demonstrated the IRA's 'technical ingenuity'. The timing mechanism, based on VCR technology at the time, and the use of a computer microchip showed the British security forces how clever the IRA had become.[3] Their logistical and technical skills had become quite sophisticated. However, Magee did leave a finger print on the cellophane that he wrapped around the bomb, according to Chalk.[4] It was this print that matched to others, including Magee's print taken many years before, that led to his eventual conviction.

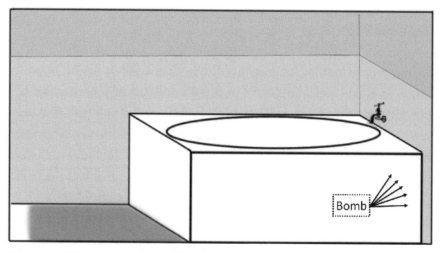

Direction of blast, towards Room 628. *(Image: created by Phil Seaman)*

When the bomb did go off, some of the impact went into the wall, which absorbed some of the explosion. At the same time, this important load-bearing wall gave way, causing the collapse as illustrated in the image on p. 42.

However, I intend to show how the bomber had got the 'right room' to stand a chance of killing Thatcher, but had put the bomb on the 'wrong side'. All the bomber Patrick Magee had to do was move the device to the other side of the bath or to the other side of the room, and the story would have been very different. Marek Kubik is a researcher in civil engineering at the TSBE Centre in Reading (Technologies for Sustainable Built Environments Centre), with a special interest in building structures. He has studied the layout of the rooms and the positioning of the bomb and concurs that it was in the wrong place. He said:

> I'd agree that the position of the bomb within the room does appear to be significant. Certainly if the hotel structure was fairly uniform inside (i.e. that particular wall was not chosen because it was uniquely weak), then positioning the bomb on the other side [left corner] of the room [629] would probably have instigated a collapse mechanism one row of rooms to the left, across towards room 630, which (being taller) would be under a greater burden and would more readily collapse.[5]

Kubik's analysis substantiates the theory that a bomb in the opposite corner of Room 629 would have initiated a collapse of rooms under 629 and 630, straight on top of Thatcher's suite. If this bomb had have been moved a few feet across, the outcome would have been very different. Wakeham and Berry may well have survived, and the Tebbits would have escaped their serious injuries. However, Kubik argues that had the bomb been placed in the middle of the room, it may well have just blown a whole in the floor and those below, rather than a complete structural collapse. He says a corner blast was needed to take out two supporting walls, to have a better chance of destabilising the structure. He also notes the lack of a central load-bearing wall under Thatcher's suite, which probably would not have survived a collapse.[6] Kubik's comments show that had the bomb been planted on the other side of the room, possibly just on the other side of the bath tub, the collapse would probably have been shifted to the left, possibly killing Thatcher.

Structural engineer Jon Orrell, of Hemsley Orrell Partnership in Hove, was in Brighton at the time and has studied this theory as well. Orrell complicates it further by arguing that 'the further an explosive device is from a wall or some such, then the least the effect. Covering over or containing an explosion … is a good way of making it more powerful'.[7] In other words, he thinks that the bomb was more powerful 'because' it was up against a wall. Independent ballistics expert Frank Lawton also studied this theory, but could not agree. He thinks Magee got a room wherever he could and worked out that a supporting wall under a chimney stack would have had maximum destructive potential. Therefore, Magee purposely puts the device on that side of the room. To back up his theory, Lawton, cites a study by Peter Gurney, a former Metropolitan Police explosives officer who investigated the Brighton bomb. In Gurney's book about worldwide bomb attacks, *Braver Men Walk Away*, he says 'damage and death had been caused not so much by the bomb's power as its position. The collapse of the hotel's central flooring system was due entirely to the weight of the chimney crashing through from the roof to the ground level.'[8] It is a logical argument that the bomber Patrick Magee would have wanted to create as much damage as possible. There are similarities to my argument and Gurney's. He insists the position of the bomb was crucial.[9] He focuses on the positioning of the chimney stack as the part that caused the damage. He insists that buildings can cope with downward thrusts better than upward thrusts.[10] The explosion went up, hit the huge chimney stack which then plummeted downwards at an alarming rate. I maintain that given a better trajectory the bomb would have done this as well as taking out walls on either side. The wall that it hit, to a certain extent, acted as a cushion. This goes against the views of structural engineer Jon Orrell who believes the complete opposite.

However, I maintain my argument that if he had known by planting the bomb on the opposite side of the room he may have destroyed less of the building, but increased his chances of getting Margaret Thatcher, then he would most certainly have moved the device.

When discussing this with Chief Constable Simon Parr, a young constable on duty that morning, he also raises the point that one of the reasons the rubble and debris took the route it did was because it was placed next to a wall that was joined onto the chimney, with debris following the path of least resistance through the chimney network. Parr also brings up two other interesting points. The first being it was the Thursday night, therefore the last night of the conference, and therefore a number of delegates were out of bed and in the ballroom celebrating and therefore not in their rooms when the blast happened. He suggests that if it had been the Tuesday or Wednesday or even a few hours later then more people may have been affected. Indeed, a combination of these small differences could well have changed the entire outcome of the explosion. In other words, Magee not only got the wrong side of the room but he got the wrong day as well. Either way, he had come very close to achieving his objective.

Chapter 18

The Security Issue

As with any study of a terrorist attack, the issue of security is always crucial. Here, we need to assess the failings of the security immediately before the Brighton bomb. Writing for the *Sunday Telegraph* as the twentieth anniversary of the bombing approached, Michael Portillo said the news events of 2004 reminded him of what he called 'the farcical lack of security in Brighton before the attack'.[1] He was of course referring to Batman scaling the walls of Buckingham Palace, hunt protesters storming Parliament and a journalist walking into Parliament with a model bomb. Portillo reminded readers of how bedroom keys were left in pigeonholes at the entrance to the hotel. He also claimed that they were often left unattended. Portillo worked for Nigel Lawson, the Chancellor of the Exchequer, at the time of the bomb and was staying in a nearby hotel that night. But he claims to have been able to deliver papers to Lawson's room by helping himself to the key, unchallenged. Portillo went on to ridicule a BBC documentary that praised Sussex Police for their faultless investigation and swift arrest. Therefore when Palace and Parliament have been blown up said Portillo, 'we can look forward to an effective inquiry leading to an arrest. It is consoling to know.'[2]

Roger Birch was the Chief Constable of Sussex Police at the time of the bombing. The night before the explosion and what was to be the final day of the conference, Home Secretary Leon Brittan and Roger Birch met up and Brittan thanked him for the police assistance and protection throughout the conference. Birch later admitted that threat levels from Special Branch and the Met often came in to be assessed; something that was quite normal. However, Birch told the media in the weeks before the conference, that the threat level, and especially the IRA threat level, was not that high. No intelligence suggested that an attack on this scale was imminent. Nobody suspected what was about to happen. The fatal explosion occurred just hours after the ironic discussion between Brittan and Birch.

In the House of Lords four days after the explosion, Deputy Prime Minister Lord Whitelaw, stated that total security can never be achieved. He said:

> I have already made known my own view that total, impregnable security is not compatible with the free society we enjoy. We must continue to search for improvements in security arrangements but without calling into question the entire basis upon which public life in this country is conducted. I can assure your Lordships that the circumstances of this outrage are being studied with meticulous care and the security implications will be explored to the full.[3]

Gary McGladdery says the bomb in Room 629 had to be just high enough to avoid detection, but also close enough to get to the Prime Minister. He says Patrick Magee took advantage of the lax security at the time.[4] Security was not good in general at the 1984 conference, and a number of fundamental errors were made. Alex Carlisle, the MP for Montgomery, reminded the House of Commons on 22 January 1985 that two weeks before the conference Metropolitan police officers searched the first floor of the hotel, where Cabinet ministers were to stay, and 'forgot' to check the room allocated to the Home Secretary.[5] On that day in January 1985, Home Secretary Leon Brittan addressed the House of Commons in relation to the Hoddinott Report. This report and investigation into security surrounding Brighton was directed by the Deputy Chief Constable of Hampshire, Sir John Hoddinott. Leon Brittan told the House:

> Mr. Hoddinott paid particular attention to search procedures. He did not criticise the police for failing to control and search each person entering the hotel during the period of the conference. He concluded

that the hotel would not have accepted such an arrangement and that, given the assumption of free access to the hotel, the numbers involved would anyway have made it impracticable.

Leon Brittan recognised Hoddinott's views as follows:

- No police force would have searched the whole hotel prior to the conference
- Some rooms were not searched at all
- Sussex police should not be blamed for missing the bomb on the sixth floor[6]

Let us consider the fact that this was one police force judging and assessing another police force. Meanwhile, Brittan concluded by saying that total security was not possible but that following the bombing security should be increased. In response, the MP for Manchester, Gorton, Gerald Kaufman told the House he was particularly concerned by the admission that rooms of key politicians, including that of the Home Secretary himself, had simply not been searched and in theory a bomb on the first floor may well have gone undetected as much as the one on the sixth floor had. Kaufman's main point was that a more thorough search should have taken place.[7] Kaufman admitted that searching everyone as they entered the hotel might not have been practical but some random bag searches may have helped tighten security, just as this type of procedure does at various shops and places of entertainment.[8] Leon Brittan told the House that while Mr Hoddinott's conclusion was that Sussex Police made proper plans and put them into force competently he did criticise the inadequacy of co-operation between police and hotel management.

Hoddinott also found fault with the lack of communication within the force when it came to establishing search requirements and threat levels. He was critical of the inadequate search of the first floor of the hotel. One other point from Hoddinott that Brittan reported to the House on 22 January 1985 was that security at the conference centre itself could have been improved. The Home Secretary told the House that 'In the light of Brighton we must enhance previously acceptable levels of security and equip ourselves to take in a clear-sighted way the difficult decisions involved in making any changes in the balance between security and the conduct of politics in a free society.'[9] Southampton MP James Hill told the House that one of the most crucial areas of police work came as hundreds of occupants were herded onto the promenade and that he was concerned this was not the correct thing to do because everyone was potentially together and could become victims of a second IRA bomb. In other words, if prominent people are herded together then they could become targets of new assassins.[10] Bournemouth East MP David Atkinson urged the Home Secretary to allow the Brighton bombers to face treason charges. He asked the Home Secretary if the death penalty still applied to treason cases. Leon Brittan confirmed that capital punishment in Britain still applies to treason cases but it would be inappropriate for him to comment on a case that was on-going.

During the parliamentary debate on the findings of the Hoddinott Report Bolsover MP Dennis Skinner challenged the Home Secretary about the hours Sussex Police spent on the miners' strike and how it was hypocritical to sort out what went wrong in October 1984 but not the miners' dispute that took up lots of police man hours. The Surbiton MP Richard Tracey asked Leon Brittan whether the report discussed the implication of modern-day terrorism methods that make guaranteeing the security of important people difficult, especially when so many are in the same place at the same time, and the information is known publicly so far in advance. Peter Bruinvels, MP for Leicester East, called for the searching of individuals on entering the conference hotel in future, and for consideration over whether it is appropriate to put all senior ministers in the same hotel at the same time.

The debate continued for some hours. MPs were mostly positive about the efforts made by Sussex Police and all of them supported comments that recognised the bravery of all the emergency services involved in the search and rescue. There was, however, some dissatisfaction that only part of the Hoddinott Report was available for inspection. Some of it was not revealed immediately because of security issues. This caused some anger in the House. The debate focused on what went wrong in Brighton, and matters of security at future political events. The Home Secretary stated that 'I have … asked Her Majesty's Chief Inspector of Constabulary, Sir Lawrence Byford, to head a team of chief constables and others to prepare urgently proposals for security at this year's party conferences and comparable occasions'.[11]

One could argue that the main problem with the security over Brighton is that the authorities were watching the wrong target. G. Davidson Smith agrees, and says, 'only the Prime Minister's suite had the sniffer dogs in. Police and security advisors were more concerned about demonstrators over the miners' strike.'[12] Indeed, authorities were obsessed with possible civil disobedience incidents relating to the miners' strike, unemployment, or even the treament of IRA hunger strikers' a few years before (1981). Smith says that it turned out that police concerns over mass demonstrations were totally wrong, and in the end it was the actions of just 'one' man on his own, IRA bomber Patrick Magee, who breached security in spectacular style.[13] Security services had their concerns in the wrong place and were too late as well; Magee had been and gone weeks before the security sweeps. Police and security services were caught off-guard. This comes despite the fact that certain newspapers in the United States claimed the Brighton bomb was planned for the 1983 Conservative Party Conference, but the operation was not ready on time, and British authorities had received a warning about a possible bomb in Brighton in 1984. Security services in the UK acknowledged that they had indeed received a warning, but that it was too vague and too generic. In 2004 the *Tablet*, in its article 'Unrepentant, Unforgiven', claimed that in 1984 security forces had discovered a cache of IRA equipment, including long-delay timers, and that the high national security alert was not taken into account in Brighton.[14] What security services should have worked out is the fact that the IRA traditionally carried out the biggest attacks just before their own annual meeting. A proper acknowledgement of this theory could have proved vital. It may have led to extra precautions, for example, checking all the hotel rooms, or at least all the rooms of the most senior politicians. Perhaps then, there would not have been a bomb at Brighton at all.

Just a few months before the Brighton bomb there had also been an incident involving Sinn Fein's Gerry Adams, who was shot and seriously wounded. The Sinn Fein website says, 'In 1984 he was shot and seriously wounded by a unionist death squad working in collusion with British Intelligence.'[15] Several gunmen shot Gerry Adams about twenty times in the neck, shoulder and arm. Shoppers watched in horror at the scene in Belfast as Adams and three travelling companions were attacked. Adams had been made Sinn Fein President in 1983. One man travelling with them was unhurt. Three plain-clothes police officers immediately arrested three suspects. Adams and his travelling companions were taken to hospital, and he was released after five days. Sometime after the outlawed Loyalist group, the Ulster Freedom Fighters, admitted to the shooting, describing Adams as a 'legitimate target of war', accusing him of being behind a campaign of murder against Protestants. Adams has always denied being in the IRA. He said he believed that the British army knew about the shooting and allowed it to go ahead. A few weeks before the attack Gerry Adams prophetically said he had a 90 per cent risk of being assassinated. Three men received jailed terms for the shooting.

Security officers in Brighton should have laid plans for a possible revenge attack. Adams was shot by Loyalist paramilitary John Gregg, who died in 2003. Gregg had served as brigadier of the UDA's South East Antrim Brigade. In addition, Christopher Andrew, the author of *Defence of the Realm* and an authority on MI5, told the BBC that at this time Special Branch was in charge of anti-terrorist activities, not MI5. He says that only changed after the bombing attack on Downing Street in 1991.[16] This begs the question, if MI5 had had a serious role pre-Brighton, would the attack have happened at all? Andrew argues it is MI5 that are the specialists in anti-terrorism, which is why Britain has probably escaped its own 9/11.

Channel 4's Gill Nevill suggested that attacks like Brighton would make government more isolated from the people. Thatcher denied this was the case, stating she thought that it had the opposite effect and unified them as they all had a part to play in fighting terrorism, by giving evidence, being alert, observing and being involved in a wider collective responsibility.[17] In an interview with the *Birmingham Post* on 25 October, journalist John Lewis discussed with the Prime Minister the impending Whitehall committee that was to examine security issues surrounding close contact between Ministers and MPs and the public. Thatcher was quick to point out that while having to be certain not to make life easy for the terrorists MPs had to carry on with contact with the public, despite the hazard.[18] She told a Channel 4 interview that 'we do live in a certain amount of danger and if you want to carry out your job you shall continue but we must never, never, never be stopped from going among the people by a few men of violence, because that is what they want'.[19] With every terrorist attack, there are civilian casualties, and Brighton was no different. Kevin Toolis states that by the 1970s and 1980s, the IRA was operating on two levels. He claims volunteers were used to hit soft or easy targets, and more experienced active-service units were used for the more complex terror operations. As Toolis puts it, 'there would have been a team of supporters, hiding equipment, renting accomodation etc.'.[20] Toolis's view is that the IRA Army Council had never intended to kill regular civilians, only military, economic and political targets were seen as legitimate. He argues the IRA knew and accepted, with regret, regular people would get in the way.[21] The IRA's line has always been that casualties are an unfortunate by-product of 'war', and that if Britain was not 'occupying' Northern Ireland, there would be no war at all.

Did the 'success' of Brighton give the IRA a taste for more senior political targets. Dr Clive Walker says 'there were more IRA incidents in 1990 than in any other year since 1975'.[22] There could have been another shot at 'the big one'. Walker claims although Brighton was the biggest political target, munitions found near Scarborough in March 1989 were also linked to a forthcoming gathering of Conservatives. Between 1988 and 1990, a number of military targets included: Inglis Barracks in London, Tern Hill Army Base in Shropshire, the Royal Marine School of Music in Deal and an army recruitment office in Wembley, as well as others. There were fatalities or injuries at all of them. One of the consequences of Brighton is the inaccessibility of ministers to the public. They are now more physically distant than ever before. They are not as accessible to the voters as they once were. This cannot be a good thing for democracy. Before the Brighton bombing only a handful of Cabinet ministers had round the clock police protection, for example, the Prime Minister, the Home Secretary and the Northern Ireland Secretary. And after the bombing several more politicians were assigned their own police protection. Prime Ministers on the move used to have two protection cars following. Since Brighton, this has dramatically changed. There is now often a convoy of five or six cars. Brighton alerted the government to just how physically vulnerable the Prime Minister can be.

Four years later the Tories came back to Brighton for another conference. A bit like shutting the stable door after the horse has bolted, security went into overdrive. There was a curtain of steel around the conference centre, hotel and immediate buildings. It was completely ringed by armed police. It was impossible to get through. Even every member of the emergency services had to wear extra ID. There were sniffer dogs everywhere before and during the entire conference. Police officers even went to fire stations, in case fire crews were attacked and prevented from helping in an emergency. Sussex Fire & Rescue officer George Hammond, remembering having to show his ID at the check points, says the police completely overreacted with security in 1988. He said colleagues had been worried about being targets, as a punishment for rescuing Tories in 1984. Hammond says there were plans to seal all the town's water hydrants to the ground, until it was argued that this would prevent fire crews from saving the very lives of people the police were trying to save if they did weld them down.[23] Local police officer Simon Parr was involved in the 1984 conference, as well as the subsequent three Tory conferences. He says that a clear message was being sent to the community and to terrorists that the government would not back down and that life would carry on as normal. He admits that 'the creation of the island site and the search regime were hugely disruptive for a period of time and extremely expensive',[24] but insists that it allowed the conference to go ahead undisturbed. Parr says over time things changed and as policing became more sophisticated and intelligence clearer, subsequent conferences were not quite as disruptive.[25] Thatcher told the 1988 conference 'four years have passed since we last came to Brighton for our conference. We all have memories of that week: memories sad and memories brave. But the human spirit is indomitable. And today we take inspiration from those of our friends, many of them here in this hall, friends who survived to rededicate themselves to the cause of freedom.'[26]

Other security developments as a direct result of Brighton were announced by the Minister of State for the Home Office, Lord Elton, on 22 October 1984. 'Immediate attention has been given to the assessment of other potential targets and the provision of proper protection for them. I can assure the House that after appropriate discussions that the House authorities have already set in hand new measures to improve security in the Palace of Westminster. The Brighton bombing also demonstrates the vulnerability of party political engagements.'[27]

- Better security awareness at all political engagements
- Improved security at Westminister
- Development of a Parliamentary Security Committee to assess intelligence

There is no question that security around politicians stepped up post-Brighton. In fact, Patrick Magee was caught six months after, when he was followed and in June 1985 had planted another long-delay timer on a bomb at the Rubens Hotel, near Buckingham Palace. Post-Brighton diligence cannot be faulted, after detectives examined the 3,798 dustbins of evidence from the Grand Hotel and 46,000 tonnes of debris loaded onto trucks. That's how they discovered the new long-delay bomb method.[28]

Chapter 19

The Man Who Planted the Bomb – Patrick Magee

'No one is born a terrorist'. Poignant words from Jo Berry, the daughter of Sir Anthony Berry MP who died in the Brighton bombing. Magee has publicly said that he regrets the loss of life but stands by the bombing. Magee is quoted as saying 'I will always carry the burden that I harmed other human beings. But I'm not seeking forgiveness.'[1] Jo Berry says the term forgiveness can be rather condescending and creates a culture of 'them' and 'us'.[2] Magee is quoted as saying 'no matter what we can achieve as two human beings meeting after a terrible event, the loss remains and forgiveness can't embrace that loss.'[3] Jo Berry told the *Haaretz* newspaper in 2013 that she began to see the human face of Patrick Magee and that the image of the terrorist faded, replaced by the image of a man.[4] He stated that all avenues had been closed to them and therefore the only recourse was to take part in violent conduct.[5] Soon after his release under the Good Friday Agreement in 1998 Patrick Magee and Jo Berry formed a working friendship where they promote dialogue and mutual understanding as a way of addressing conflict around the world. Berry and Magee run an organisation called Building Bridges for Peace, promoting peace and conflict resolution throughout the world. Lynne J. Cameron says the Berry/Magee conversations are extraordinary in that they show 'responses to violence and conflict that avoid revenge and bitterness'.[6] Magee says he refuses to believe he is a violent person.[7] On the Building Bridges website Magee says about Jo Berry, 'It is rare to meet someone as gracious and open as Jo … that is a very humbling experience'.[8] Their relationship was featured in a BBC documentary, *Facing the Enemy* (2001). In addition, a film called *Soldiers of Peace* (2009) features stories of conflict resolution around the world. On the website buildingbridgesforpeace.org, Jo Berry, referring to the death of her father in the explosion, states:

> I made a personal decision … to bring something positive out of this emotionally shattering trauma and to try and understand those who had killed him. I chose to give up blame and revenge, instead taking responsibility for my pain and feelings, transforming them into passion for peace. The journey of healing began with my intention and I trusted that life would then bring me the opportunities to heal and grow.[9]

Jo Berry said that the hardest bridge to build was with Patrick Magee. She finally met him for the first time in November 2000, in Dublin, so she could hear his story and see him as a human rather than a faceless enemy. Jo said she could see he was sensitive and intelligent as he talked about his political approach to it all. However, he stopped talking and said he did not know who he was anymore and asked what he could do to help. Jo Berry saw this as a turning point; the junction where Magee took off his political hat (according to Berry) and really opened up. From here, she claims that the conversation changed and a new journey started.

Patrick Magee, Harvey Thomas (Thatcher's former Director of Communications who was injured in the explosion) and Jo Berry have all since become friends. Jo Berry was keen for something positive to come out of the atrocity. She and Magee met at a house in Dublin and talked for three hours. Jo Berry said it was important to channel any anger she had to fight for change. In 1998 Harvey Thomas took the decision, as a Christian he says, to write to Patrick Magee and forgive him for what he had done. Magee said he agreed to the meeting from a political obligation to explain his motivation about being involved in an armed conflict. Magee told one independent documentary maker, Andy Anderson, while referring to it as armed conflict and war, 'you have a reduced view of people you call your enemy and see only the uniform or the political label or nationality'. He said that he, Berry and Thomas would never agree politically but he agreed to the meeting to talk but on the assurance that it was not confrontational.[10]

Many people see forgiveness as an important part of moving forward. Former Middle-East hostage Terry Waite once said, 'A part of the key to entering into forgiveness, is understanding. If one can understand why people behave as they do then often the road to forgiveness is opened ... bitterness is like a cancer that enters the soul.'[11]

Patrick Magee has never asked for forgiveness, saying what he did was a conscionable decision. He seeks understanding and dialogue to prevent conflict in the future getting out of hand. However, it is a known fact that the UK government and the IRA had unofficial meeting channels that were not made public. To analyse the significance or contribution of these meetings to the overall peace process is impossible. The point is that these unofficial meetings were dialogue, albeit brief and unofficial.

Elsewhere, in 1993 a young America woman called Amy Biehl was killed in South Africa during a riot. The tragedy was documented in a film called *Long Night's Journey into Day* in 2000. British writer and broadcaster Simon Fanshawe was interested in how the film presented the Truth and Reconciliation Commission in post-apartheid South Africa and he travelled there to meet Amy's parents. They had actually been instrumental in the running of the Truth and Reconciliation Commission. Subsequently, Fanshawe got involved with the Forgiveness Project that accepts conflict is a given and it is the response that matters. Fanshawe insists that this attitude 'roots them [Berry and Magee] in a strong reality'. He says 'it is not about getting an apology, it is about getting heard – that's more realistic'. In 2003 Simon Fanshawe chaired a public debate at the Institute for Contemporary Art in London and met Jo Berry. They discussed what they might be able to do for the approaching twentieth anniversary of the bombing. Simon, a great believer in the inevitability of conflict, claims, 'you can't avoid it; you are in a fool's paradise if you think you can'.[12] Of course there is a time and place for prevention and punishment, argues Simon, but there is also something beyond that: restorative justice, dialogue, reconciliation.

In 2004 Simon Fanshawe and Jo Berry decided to hold a public discussion, involving Patrick Magee. Simon was attacked in the press for supporting the event, the police had to carry out a risk assessment and the venue was kept secret until the last moment. Audience members were emailed the venue details just hours before. On that first public discussion Fanshawe said:

I moderated the first conversation in public between Patrick Magee, the Brighton bomber, and Jo Berry, whose father he killed. You cannot 'agree' about a murder. But Jo persists in trying to understand Patrick's motives and reasons and he persists in trying to face up to the human consequences of his actions. He doesn't apologise and she doesn't ask him to. But they have a genuine dialogue. It enables them to manage (and build) a relationship.[13]

However, five years later Simon said everything had changed when he helped organise a similar public question and answer session with Berry and Magee at the Duke of York Picturehouse in Brighton. He said he received letters of support from members of the public and suffered no vicious attacks in the press, apart from some tabloids which he dismissed. He still cannot work out why attitudes changed so dramatically in those five years. Time is naturally a great healer, but that much, in that little time? asks Simon. One reason he offers is that Patrick Magee and Jo Berry have talked consistently, openly and publicly about their work, year in, year out and people's attitudes to resolution may have changed.

Furthermore, on the matter of apologising, Simon reiterates that Patrick Magee has never publicly apologised to Jo Berry for killing her father. He takes responsibility and says he is reminded of the hurt and pain. Simon believes that as the two of them listen intently to each other, an apology would almost weaken the dialogue. It is more about listening and understanding, which is even deeper. All along, Jo Berry wanted an explanation, not an apology, and wanted to understand. She felt that if she grasped these elements then her father's death may not have been in vain. Her desire to understand the reasons behind what happened have always been paramount.

Magee acknowledged the fact that it is difficult to sit with someone whose father he killed. He admitted that despite the political reasons every time he meets Jo the fact that he killed her father is at the forefront of his mind and he cannot hide behind the politics. In this frank interview Jo Berry admits that Patrick took off his political hat and even shed a tear. Over the years Jo says that Patrick has never shirked away from the times she has been angry or upset. Patrick said it would have been easier to deal with anger than someone who was prepared to listen. Jo says her relationship and discussions with Patrick have helped her understand why people around the world have at times resorted to violence. Magee made reference to the political, social and economic barriers and how being marginalised was difficult. Jo finished the meeting by saying that it had meant a lot to her to sit and listen to the man who had killed her father and that it could only bring something positive out of what had happened in 1984. The bombing in Brighton was at the height of the political conflict, what was described as an 'ethno-sectarian conflict'.[14] Journalists reported one Protestant bishop who said it was caused by 'unresolved tensions between two competing communities, from a time when politics and religion were inseparably linked'.[15]

Magee was a special guest at the House of Commons on the twenty-fifth anniversary of the bombing, in October 2009. The ex-IRA bomber was speaking alongside Jo Berry during the visit. Berry likened it to Guy Fawkes being invited to Parliament. The meeting was organised by MPs to aid reconciliation, the All-Party Parliamentary Group on Conflict Issues.

Berry told the *Guardian* newspaper that she wanted to show MPs what war is about, and that humanising the enemy is important to try and stop violence. She claimed that nobody is born a terrorist.[16] The *Mirror* newspaper reported that Magee had remained defiant during the visit and on the subject of becoming a terrorist apparently said that he did not think he could have made a different choice.[17] The *Daily Mail* ran the headline 'Killer in the Commons'.[18] Many were outraged at the invitation, including Lord Tebbit who claimed Magee had never shown any regret or named those who supplied him with the explosives to carry

The House of Commons where Magee was a guest. *(Photo: Abby White)*

out the atrocity. The *Heraldscotsman* also ran a story on the meeting at the Commons, with comments from Sir Donald Maclean. Maclean, whose wife was murdered in the IRA blast, said Patrick Magee remained 'cowardly and unrepentant'. He claimed that the meeting would only generate 'publicity for the wrong people'.[19]

Maclean, 79, was president of the Scottish Conservative & Unionist Association when the bomb intended to kill Margaret Thatcher and her Cabinet exploded at the Grand Hotel.

At the same time as the visit to the Commons, Noman Tebbit was making a speech at the hospital where his wife Margaret was still being treated for her injuries. Tebbit reminded the press that he lost five of his friends at the hands of Patrick Magee. Lord Tebbit told the *Belfast Telegraph* that allowing Magee to ask for forgiveness while he remains unrepentant is the equivalent of hoisting up a flag for terrorists.[20] Phil Good, founder and director of the Forgiveness Project, said that he was not surprised by the

Simon Fanshawe hosting a public discussion about conflict and dialogue with Magee and Berry on stage with him, Brighton, 2009. The author was present. *(Photo: Kieran Hughes)*

reaction of some people, branding the visit to the House of Commons as a stunt. The day after Magee visited the House of Commons the *Sun* newspaper ran the headline: 'Bomber Defiance – The ex-IRA man, freed under the Good Friday Agreement, said he was not "sorry" for the Tory conference attack in 1984 which killed five people – but did have "regret".'[21]

Magee makes regular speeches about conflict resolution. The reception he receives varies from place to place and he has not always been received in a calm or diplomatic manner. In January 2014 he was due to give a talk at a community centre in East Belfast. About fifty people had gathered outside the venue and there was a heavy police presence. Some protestors threw stones and fireworks and four police officers were injured, although officers

Simon Fanshawe, who still has a busy working relationship with Magee and Berry.

managed to hold the protestors back. Magee and Berry were forced to go in together through a rear door so they could take part in a festival called 'Listening to Your Enemies'.[22]

At the start of April 2014 Northern Ireland's Deputy First Minister Martin McGuinness went to a banquet at Windsor Castle and joined in a toast to the Queen. It was a far cry from his days as a Sinn Fein MP when he refused to sit in the House of Commons because he would have had to swear an oath of allegiance to the monarch. In the words of *Daily Telegraph* journalists Christopher Hope and James Kirkup, Martin McGuinness was a man who once wore a black balaclava as a commando of the IRA, an organisation that murdered members of the Royal Family to try and end the authority of the British Crown in Ireland.[23] Here he was on Tuesday, 8 April, dining with the Queen and toasting her health and happiness.

Not everyone was happy at his appearance. Relatives of IRA victims protested outside the castle, including Victor Baker, whose 12-year-old son died in the Omagh bombing in 1998. He held a sign that said: 'A terrorist in a white tie and tails is still a terrorist – Martin McGuiness [*sic*] time to tell the truth'. In addition, the sister of a woman killed in the Birmingham pub bombings in 1974 called for McGuinness to be arrested. While the Queen talked of Britain and Ireland moving on from the past, the Irish President said that those who had died or were bereaved or injured during the conflict should also be remembered. Victor Baker is not the only one who found it difficult to embrace changes in this field. Michael Dobbs, Thatcher's former aide who was in the Grand Hotel when it was bombed, says he finds it difficult to be in the same room as Gerry Adams and Martin McGuinness and feels drawn to the exit.[24]

In 1999 Patrick Magee was freed from prison after serving fourteen years of his life sentence. Many other paramilitaries were also let out as part of the Good Friday Agreement. Lord Jenkin points out that 'the early release scheme was an important part of the Peace Process and must have been very difficult for the relatives of the victims to accept, but without that concession there would have been no Peace Process'.[25] Since his release from prison Magee has at times expressed remorse for his victims. But he defends his actions as part of a military struggle. He described his political victims to me as legitimate targets, while expressing regret at the loss of human life. His statements, put together and studied, are rather discombobulating. He certainly does not seek forgiveness, saying, 'I would not ask people to forgive, why should they? Just the understanding is all I could hope for.'[26]

The biggest discussion surrounding the Brighton Bomber Patrick Magee is 'regret'. Is he sorry for planting the bomb and causing death? I met Magee in two different surroundings. The first time was a discussion in a busy pub in St Pancras, London. I felt that he was keen on engineering the discussion to take place in daylight, with many people around. He would not move to a quieter area which would have been the logical thing to do as it was very noisy in the bar. Incredibly, I thought, nobody in the pub recognised him. To prove this, I asked a nearby dining couple to take a picture of us, to which they asked if we were enjoying our 'holiday'. I found Magee quite guarded as he checked out my university ID badge and refused a drink. The *Haaretz* newspaper described Magee as more 'closed, rigid and inscrutable' than Jo Berry.[27]

Having met Patrick Magee privately and also listened to his public discussion at the event in Brighton, I was of the opinion that there was an element of unintentional contradiction on the issue of saying sorry. This can be analysed by comparing my notes from both sessions. Examples are as follows:

My questions, on a one-to-one basis:

Q: 'Are you sorry for what you did?'
A: 'I stand by my actions, I can regret my actions, but I thought what I was doing at the time was right … I did.'

Question at the public debate:

Q: 'Are you sorry?'
A: 'How can I not be sorry?'[28]

He went on to say how he killed and injured people, and left one in a wheelchair (a reference to Margaret Tebbit).

Here's another example. Magee at the public debate:

'Now we can more openly talk about the past.'

Magee challenged in a one-to-one interview with me over not revealing who gave the orders for the attack in Brighton said, 'The Government has remained tight-lipped about its actions in Northern Ireland, so I will too.' Magee said that he was doing a job and was not privy to that kind of information.

One could argue that this is proof there is a lot we still do not know about the Brighton bombing. We still do not know exactly who ordered the execution of the Prime Minister, and how it was planned. Probably only a handful of former IRA operatives were privy to these secrets. There is obviously a list of possible contenders but Magee is certainly not going to spill the beans now. He has served his prison sentence and there is nothing in it for him to share any information. But his defence in not saying anything is the comment above, about staying tight-lipped like the UK government, according to Magee. He explained this by saying that he would not have been party to any discussions higher up and that he was probably picked for the job as he was the right man around at the time.

Norman Tebbit has publicly said, on a number of occasions, that he wants these details to be made public. He was quoted in the *Daily Mail* as saying 'What I would like to hear from Mr. Magee is that he has repented his sins and he is going to the authorities to give them the names and the details of those who procured and planned, so he could carry out those murders. Magee goes around seeking forgiveness but he has not repented.'[29] When I first met Magee he looked at my list of questions about what, where, how and when in relation to the bombing operation. He ran his fingers down the page and said, over and over again 'I am not answering that, I am not answering that, I am not answering that, I am not answering that', about a dozen times. They were mainly 'operational' questions.

Magee's interview with *Haaretz* newspaper in 2013 was just as unrevealing. Journalists Gideon Levy and Nir Kafri stated that 'any attempt to pry from him details about his planning and his accomplices, who were never caught, meets with silence. Even today he will not discuss any military and operational details of IRA activities.'[30] It is this determination of secrecy that Lord Tebbit gets angry about. I would argue that it prevents a complete sense of closure and moving on, unless it is on his (Magee's) terms. This is something picked up on by BBC journalist Mark Lawson in his review of two TV documentaries on the bombing. Questioned by Peter Taylor on why he used as his pseudonym the name and address of a jailed IRA terrorist, he strangely refused to say.[31] Magee does have a record of refusing to comment on a number of issues. This was a legitimate question because using the identification of a jailed IRA man was part of the reason Magee got caught.

Meanwhile, there have been accusations for many years that Magee was trained in Libya. He strenuously denies this, saying, 'There is no truth in the Libyan training allegations. I have never even been to Libya and I have no reason to lie about that now.' Much has been written and suggested about this alleged link but Magee was determined that it played no part in his actions. Magee did, however, give me an insight into why he joined the Republican movement. He claims there was no single event that caused him to join. It was an accumulation of things. He said, 'it is hard to explain motivations, they are always complex'.[32] He also said that he saw the Republican movement as a civil rights thing, many who were contained, or were clamped down and silenced, like him, joined the IRA, he told me. He recalled being interned for four years in the early 1970s and realised there had to be some drastic action, like bombing the British establishment.[33]

Having looked at Magee's insistence that his activities had nothing to do with Libya, it is important to examine the relationship between the UK and Libya when it involved Irish Republicanism. Whether Magee's answer (given to me before Gaddafi's fall) would have been different post-Gaddafi, is impossible to say. Gaddafi's regime seized power in 1969 and supported the IRA for many years. The Republican army had been badly armed in the 1960s with old, outdated weapons, but Muammar Gaddafi perceived the IRA as a comrade-in-arms in need of his help. He was partly responsible for providing them with the modern means to fight, what he saw as, British Imperialism. In 1973 the Irish navy boarded a ship called the *Claudia*, off the Irish coast, where they discovered 5 tonnes of weaponry supplied by Libya. This was the first proven link between the two groups. Three other shipments are thought to have already got through. Tripoli continued to supply the Provisionals in their fight against the UK government. Another partial discovery of shipped arms was made in 1978.

Meanwhile, in 1973 Britain made a secret offer to pay Libya £14 million if it stopped supplying arms to the IRA, official files have revealed. The deal put forward by Harold Wilson's Labour government was also aimed at helping trade with the oil-rich state. Wilson even sent a personal message to Gaddafi suggesting the UK would make the payment – worth £500 million in today's money. There is no evidence that the money was actually paid but the correspondence illustrates a tense and precarious diplomatic relationship between the two countries.

It seems that negotiations were not particularly successful long-term because in 1987 1,000 AK-47 machine guns, 50 ground-to-air missiles and 2 tonnes of Semtex where discovered by French authorities on the Northern Ireland-bound vessel the *Eksund*. It is thought Gaddafi and the IRA links had re-emerged in 1986, after a break, following the death of more than a hundred people, including Gaddafi's adopted daughter, as a result of American bombing raids. It is believed that other shipments of arms reached Ireland before the *Esksund* was apprehended. In 2003, the BBC claimed to have made direct links with intelligence sources who confirmed that Libyan arms had greatly enhanced the IRA's effectiveness. Libyan Semtex was also used in the 1987 Enniskillen bomb and the 1988 Ballygawley bus bomb. Gaddafi was thought to be behind the

1988 bombing of Pan Am flight 103 over Lockerbie, although some have accused others.

The question remains – was Libya directly or indirectly behind the Brighton bombing of 1984? The second part of the question is far easier to answer than the first. Proving that Colonel Gaddafi handed over the cash to fund the Brighton explosives is difficult; illustrating an international framework and history that supports Libya's anti–West and pro-terrorist stance is easier. The question still remains – did Gaddafi finance the explosion at the Grand Hotel? Was Libyan money behind the attempt to bring down the UK government? Looking at the Libya vs United Kingdom situation in the year of the Brighton bombing alone, WPC Yvonne Fletcher was killed during a siege outside the Libyan Embassy in

The Yvonne Fletcher Memorial, St James's Square, London. *(Photo: Kieran Hughes)*

London. On 17 April, Britain severed diplomatic relations. On 27 April 1984, thirty Libyan diplomats left Britain.

In 1979, the Jonathan Institute was established with the aim of creating a high-profile, international anti-terrorist platform. One of its first speakers at the first meeting held in Jerusalem was American Senator Henry M. Jackson, who said, 'I believe that international terrorism is a modern form of warfare against liberal democracies. I believe that the ultimate but seldom stated goal of these terrorists is to destroy the very fabric of democracy.'[34]

By now in Jerusalem talk of state-backed terrorism became the buzzword, and it was discussed on the international platform. Countries such as Libya, Iraq, Syria, the newly transformed Iran, South Yemen and several Arab countries were discussed. At the next conference, in June 1984 in Washington DC, the international theme continued, and it was just months before the Brighton bombing. In April of that year the Chairman of the US Joint Chief of Staffs John Vessey publicly echoed Secretary of State George Shultz's very public call to tackle state-sponsored terrorism, 'we all know that Syria, Libya and Iran have active terrorist camps. Yet no-one does anything about it.'[35] George Shultz referred to state-sponsored terrorism as a weapon already being directed at the interests, values and allies of the United States.[36] Shultz's doctrine, in a nutshell, was that state-sponsored terrorism was backed by a series of nations opposed to Western democracy, and eventually linked with the Soviet Union. It is known that some of the IRA Semtex sent by Libya came from Czechoslovakia. Jason McCue, the head of the UK-based Libya Victims Initiative, acknowledges that tonnes of Semtex had been supplied by Libya from the 1980s. After the 1998 signing of the Northern Ireland peace agreement a great deal was unaccounted for when weapons and explosives were handed in. It is feared that some had fallen into the hands of splinter groups who continue the armed struggle against British rule. Following the fatal bombing of a policeman in Omagh in 2011, McCue told the Reuters News agency that he would not be surprised if Libyan Semtex had been used. Despite negotiations with Libya for compensation for IRA victims, it is not Brighton that has been on the negotiating table. This refers to pre- and post-Gaddafi talks.

Ironically, the post-Gaddafi Libyan government struggled to contain its own internal terrorism problem, fighting rival militias and al-Qaeda-linked Islamist militants. A number of Western countries considered giving aid to Libya to help combat the problem, including France. The aid package under consideration in 2013 included counter-terrorism police training assistance.

Meanwhile, during my discussions with Patrick Magee, I asked him why Brighton had been a target in 1984. He explained how the IRA wanted their struggle to be a leading news story. 'We had to deliver a sustained campaign against the British Government. It had to be over a long period of time. They wanted to take the war off the front pages, Brighton brought it back.' This sustained attack referred to by Magee may well have been linked to the planned holiday bombing campaign – with the Rubens Hotel in London as the first on the list. The plans had been discovered in the Glasgow flat where Magee had been arrested.[37] Magee was quoted in *An Phoblacht* as stating that the British looked at the IRA very differently after Brighton.[38] He claims that even the IRA itself suddenly realised how important the campaign in England was. Magee viewed Brighton as the point where the British political establishment started to take the IRA seriously.

Norman Tebbit admits it was a good opportunity for the IRA because all the country's media were there right in front of the action, but said of Magee's comments 'when I was Tory party Chairman, if I'd have had an army of terrorists willing to kill and bomb, I could have kept my party on the front pages as well'.[39] Holland, in her article about Brighton, looks at the bigger picture and says usually any IRA bomb had three main objectives:

• To sicken the British people, so they will pressure the government to withdraw
• Boost morale among Republicans in Ireland
• Garner further backing from supporters in the United States[40]

Although it is impossible to examine the whole concept of IRA terrorism in one meeting/study, I had to put to Magee that peaceful negotiations may have had some effect. His view, and that of the IRA, was one of absolute no choice. Magee said:

> I don't think we had any other option, we could only take up an armed struggle. We were never going to defeat the British Government but felt that they must live up to their responsibilities as they were the ones with the real political power. Our weakness was our lack of politics, Westminster wouldn't deal with us. It [the bombing campaign, including Brighton] focused the Tory minds on working on the problem. But you cannot build a middle ground in politics and exclude the margins [Republicans]. If there had been direct rule earlier, it would have been much better.[41]

Magee remains angry that, in his view, the UK government has not come under scrutiny for their part in the conflict and the supplying of weapons to Republican opponents. He claims the focus has always been on the IRA. What was going through Magee's mind before, during and after the bombing in Brighton? Nowhere has this ever been fully examined before. No book has been published on the attack. Most books on terrorism and the IRA only briefly mention it and some former Conservative MPs' autobiographies pay a little attention to it, except Margaret Thatcher's and Norman Tebbit's. Magee's comments to the *Sunday Post* were reported in *An Phoblacht*, saying that that he regretted the deaths at Brighton but that the Tory ruling class could not be immune from their actions. He complained that the British dealt with the IRA through containment and criminalisation.

I asked Magee about thinking about the consequences of planting the bomb, and from his answers you can see how to him, and perhaps to the IRA, it was 'just a job'. It seems as though killing people was nothing personal, as strange as it sounds. Magee told me, 'I was focused on the job in hand, not the consequences of what I was doing. That part was put out of my mind, the focus of the job was on my mind, nothing else was going through it, I was single minded, I had to be.'[42] Magee said on that morning, when the world was waking up to the news of the bombing, he too was watching the TV, in Cork, away from the bombing scene. He said he had to make sure it had gone off. He felt relief that he had fulfilled his aim and that he had not ruined the once chance he had to get them.[43]

I asked how his thoughts had changed as he has got older. He said his focus has changed, his views (political) have not changed, but he is more conscionable. He is adamant that politicians should look to resolve conflicts rather than go down the path of violence and to understand where there are other options. Anyone in conflict should re-examine the past and learn from it, Magee stated.

Magee comes across as a serious and tough character, but I got the impression that what you see is what you get. He won't compromise on his political views. He stands by his actions. Although he regrets what happened, he won't come forward and say 'sorry' because he feels the UK government has never said sorry for its part in the Northern Ireland atrocities (his words). He also feels coming forward and publicly saying 'sorry' would add to the grief of those concerned.[44] I put it to Patrick Magee that he has more to say about the Brighton bombing, more background information, more details about the planning and strategy that he keeps locked away. He refused to comment further. He remains committed to his view that he was involved in military combat and an armed struggle. However, as Party Chairman in 1984 John Gummer later said, 'What had Tony Berry done to deserve this end? What had Roberta Wakeham done to deserve this end? This was no military action. This was a cowardly terrorist act.'[45]

Chapter 20

Norman Tebbit

There are two iconic images of the Brighton bombing. One is of the huge destruction of the wedding cake facade of the actual building after it crumbled in the explosion. The second image is that of Norman Tebbit being stretchered out of the rubble by rescue crews. A few lines in Tebbit's autobiography sums up his post-Brighton personal feelings a few weeks after Brighton, 'Realising it was best not to contemplate [his wife] Margaret's future or how we would cope if she remained severely disabled, I immersed myself in work as a prophylactic against bouts of misery and self-pity.'[1] Firefighter George Hammond said it was obvious the Tebbits were badly injured, but the rescue was made difficult because it was so dark and the electric supply had been taken out. The fire crews had to arrange for complete silence so they could listen out for the moans of trapped people. That's how they located John Wakeham. They also found Anthony Berry but it was too late for him, he had died. It must have been a frightening experience for the MP, because he had clung on to a concrete pillar when the floor gave way, and he was still clinging on to the pillar when he hit the ground and died. Fire crews had to cover up the deceased while they rescued the injured to stop them getting distressed.[2]

Surely Magee feels bad about what he has done to the Tebbits? Magee told me:

I am not sure what Tebbit wants from me, I know he has a lot of anger and I'm not sure if an apology would solve his problems. He has not recognised any legitimacy towards our struggle. The British Government took very hard actions against Northern Ireland. He should be left to deal with his grief and I don't want to add to that.[3]

In a 2004 BBC documentary, *The Hunt for the Bomber*, Patrick Magee is unrepentant over what happened but has regrets about the paralysis of Mrs Tebbit'.[4] Thirty years on Lady Tebbit is still in a wheelchair, still needing care and still requiring hospital treatment. But the Tebbits are known to be grateful they survived and had all those years together after the bombing. But it was my two-hour one-to-one meeting with Lord Tebbit in the House of Lords to discuss Brighton that was the most revealing. Over a cup of tea and a sticky bun in Parliament's canteen, Tebbit told me his personal thoughts about Magee, the bombing and the IRA. 'It's OK,' he reassured me, 'you can leave your coat on the peg in the hallway, it'll be safe, Peter Mandelson is busy debating at the moment.'

Tebbit says Magee should 'either repent or not repent. He's committed a sin. His only regret is that he didn't kill me. You can't forgive an

Lord Tebbit and the author, House of Lords, London, November 2009. *(Photo: Kieran Hughes)*

unrepentant sinner.' He calls Magee an irrelevant low-grade hit man, a monkey who does not matter. But he says there is plenty of unfinished business with the former IRA killer. Tebbit is determined Magee should come forward with details of who was on the IRA council that planned and gave the order to blow up the Grand Hotel. Despite the enormity of the bombing, Lord Tebbit told me there is a danger of overrating the incident. He was quick to point out that far fewer people died than in a tragedy like 9/11. He argues that the 1991 mortar bomb attack on John Major's Cabinet at No. 10 was close to being far more of a spectacle.[5]

Meeting Norman Tebbit (now Lord Tebbit) in person allowed me to appreciate his real feelings about Brighton, not lines in a book or interview in a newspaper. Referring to Magee as an IRA monkey, he was shaking his head and denying the bombing had any effect on the government's stance on Northern Ireland, or that it hurt the political machinery. As you would expect, he was adamant on these matters. He said Republican terrorists knew they were on the back foot when Airey Neave was lined up as a Northern Ireland Secretary (assassinated in 1979). He was a no-nonsense, hard-line politician who would have beaten the cause and clamped down on it with an iron fist, according to Tebbit.[6]

Chapter 21

The Ban on Republican Voices in the Media

In 1988, following one of the bloodiest episodes in the history of the Troubles, and four years after the Brighton bombing, the Conservative government announced that organisations in Northern Ireland suspected of supporting terrorist activities would be banned from directly broadcasting on the airwaves. The government said it was concerned about supporters of terrorism using broadcasting facilities for their own gains and how that had to be stopped. On 19 October 1988, Home Secretary Douglas Hurd said, 'for some time, broadcast coverage of events in Northern Ireland has included the occasional appearance of representatives of paramilitary organisations and their political wings, who have used these opportunities as an attempt to justify their criminal activities. Such appearances have caused widespread offence to viewers and listeners throughout the United Kingdom, particularly just after a terrorist outrage.'[1] The government said it was time to deny this easy platform to supporters of terrorism. It meant that instead of hearing Gerry Adams, viewers and listeners would hear an actor's voice reading a transcript of the Sinn Fein leader's words. Broadcast organisations kept a list of actors who could be on called at short notice.

Sinn Fein was the main target of the ban but in total eleven Loyalist and Republican organisations were affected. Hurd announced:

I have today issued to the chairmen of the BBC and the IBA a notice, under the licence and agreement and under the Broadcasting Act 1987 respectively, requiring them to refrain from broadcasting direct statements by representatives of organisations proscribed in Northern Ireland and Great Britain and by representatives of Sinn Fein ... and the Ulster Defence Association. The notices will also prohibit the broadcasting of statements by any person which support or invite support for these organisations.[2]

Not everyone was in favour of this ban on voices. Roy Hattersley, MP for Sparkbrook, Birmingham, said the move was just about preventing personal appearances and would not damage or defeat terrorism at all. Hattersley asked 'has he weighed that publicity coup for the IRA against the advantage of keeping its representatives off television?'. Opposition also came from Liberal MP Paddy Ashdown, calling it an 'IRA propaganda coup'. Ashdown was concerned about human rights and freedom of speech. He called the action 'ill-conceived, ill-judged and almost certainly counter-productive'.[3]

Sinn Fein thought that the broadcasting restrictions were an attempt by the government to silence its campaign. The director of publicity for the party at the time, Danny Morrison, said there was a lot of confusion when this ruling came out, later calling the ban a weapon of war. In later years Lord Tebbit said that the British public found the appearance of Sinn Fein leaders rather offensive and that media coverage gave the IRA publicity that it should never have had. In response to his critics, Hurd said, 'this step will provoke an immediate flurry of protest from Sinn Fein and the supporters of terrorism, but it will deny them a weapon of which I believe they have made substantial use'.[4]

Seamus Mallon, MP for Newry and Armagh asked this question to Douglas Hurd, 'would the Secretary of State care to speculate about how many of the hard-line activists in West Belfast, South Armagh and Derry will lay down their guns because they cannot watch Gerry Adams on television?'.[5] The late veteran Labour MP Tony Benn, member for Chesterfield, was against the ban and told Hurd 'any attack on the rights of elected representatives has always historically been seen as an attack upon those who elect them, the people who have chosen to use the ballot to express their views'.[6]

Brent East MP Ken Livingstone voiced his concerns over the ban, suggesting that it was a diversion from solving the real issues – asking:

How was it that the IRA managed to sustain itself, decade after decade, from the 1922 bombing campaign through into the 1930s and 1950s, without access to television? Is this not simply a diversion in response to the increased level of violence ... rather than dealing with the real problem, which is to find the answer to the violence, either by defeating terrorism, or by negotiating a peace settlement?[7]

In the United States, according to the *Chicago Tribune*, Michael Grade, Chief Executive of Channel 4, said that the ban was:

One of the most ludicrous, outrageous and pointless restrictions on free speech ever imposed in a democracy ... the idea that representatives of legal political parties, elected by proper democratic processes in part of the UK cannot be heard in their own voices on British television is frankly an international embarrassment ...[8]

The restrictions were lifted in 1994 after the announcement by the IRA of a ceasefire. At the same time, Prime Minister John Major declared that a number of major roads linking Northern Ireland with the Irish Republic that had been closed on security grounds would now reopen.

Chapter 22

In Print and in the Media –
Brushing it Under the Carpet?

Why is there so little written on the Brighton bombing of 1984? There are many books already in print about 9/11, for example, and plenty written about all manner of terrorism, both here and abroad. The incident has been deliberately swept under the carpet. The vast majority of books on the IRA and Irish terrorism ignore the Brighton bombing, or give it only a brief mention. There could be many reasons for the lack of literature on the subject. Some may see it as giving the IRA more publicity or recognition. One only has to look at the autobiographies of the senior Tories of the time to see a pattern of denial. With the exception of Thatcher and Tebbit, Tories have denied Brighton the open discussion it deserves. This chart shows the minimal coverage given by each former Tory in his memoirs – measurements are approximate:[1]

Author	Length of Memoir	Text Devoted to Brighton Bombing
John Major	790 pages	2 paragraphs
Willie Whitelaw	280 pages	No mention
John Nott	402 pages	No mention
Keith Joseph	458 pages	1 paragraph
Edward Heath	767 pages	1 paragraph
Michel Heseltine	562 pages	1 paragraph
Geoffrey Howe	736 pages	2½ pages
Douglas Hurd	472 pages	1 page
Norman Lamont	567 pages	No mention
Cecil Parkinson	312 pages	1 line
Margaret Thatcher	914 pages	7 pages
Norman Tebbit	280 pages	10 pages

In Heseltine's thirteen lines, he finished by saying, 'By a miracle they failed. The conference carried on. The Government carried on. It was business as usual: Britain at its best.'[2] In fairness Hesleltine was not there at the time but he must have strong opinions on what happened and how it affected politics, or not. He declined to be interviewed for this book. Foreign Secretary Geoffrey Howe was on the same floor as Thatcher, in the suite next door, and underneath the Tebbits. He acknowledged, 'Had I been at my desk an hour later, as I had been the night before, I should almost certainly have died'.[3] I would add that if the bomb had been a number of pounds heavier then the chimney stack collapse may have travelled down further and killed the Howes.

Meanwhile, in broadcast media, Channel 4's *Secret History, Brighton Bomb* (Mentor Productions) aired on 15 May 2003. Journalist Simon Hoggart reviewed the documentary in the *Spectator* and criticised the fact that only a small number of people had been interviewed. Hoggart claimed that 'on the whole the programme looked like an opportunity missed'.[4] BBC One produced *The Brighton Bomb* and *The Hunt for the Bomber* (two linked documentaries, 2004). Referring to Patrick Magee, journalist Mark Lawson said it was 'a bold decision to give BBC airtime to a man whose crime still has many living victims', although he said the bomber was given a tough time by the interviewer, Peter Taylor.

Chapter 23

The Good Friday Agreement

A fter almost two years of talks, thirty years of conflict and the loss of countless lives, the Northern Ireland peace talks ended on 10 April 1998 with a historic agreement. It ended decades of sectarian violence and political stalemate. Negotiations had continued for hours after the deadline for an agreement had passed. Prime Minister Tony Blair and Ireland's Prime Minister Bertie Ahern faced the press soon after negotiations had finished.

Reactions were as follows:

'I see a great opportunity for us to start a healing process.'
                              David Trimble, Ulster Unionist Leader

'Today I hope that the burden of history can at long last start to be lifted from our shoulders.'
                                        Prime Minister Tony Blair

The Irish Prime Minister Bertie Ahern said he hoped a line could be drawn under the 'bloody past'.

Sinn Fein President Gerry Adams said a gap of distrust remained between Nationalists and Unionists that 'must be bridged on the basis of equality'. He reminded others that 'we are here reaching out the hand of friendship'.

A referendum by the people north and south of the border overwhelmingly backed the Agreement. There were disagreements over arms decommissioning for the first few years and a number of suspensions of the Agreement. The Northern Ireland Assembly was suspended between 2002 and 2007 over allegations of IRA intelligence-gathering inside the Northern Ireland Office. Devolved power was restored on 8 May 2007.

Martin Mansergh said that 'progress was underpinned by the acceptance of the end of violence and of democratic means to self-determinism'. He went on to say that 'the overwhelming public desire for peace in both Northern Ireland and the Republic was perhaps the most critical factor of all'. And that 'any remaining public tolerance of continuing paramilitary atrocities was sharply diminishing'.[1]

Conclusion

Tory Peer Lord Stockton told me 'Britain's political landscape would be unrecognisable had the IRA succeeded in Brighton. Thatcher's successor may well have lost the next election. Neil Kinnock may have been elected and probably failed, and that means there would probably have been no Tony Blair in power. The ramifications of that, amongst many, may have been no war in Afghanistan or Iraq.'[1] More of the what-ifs are discussed in the following pages.

But there remains another burning question: does terrorism work? One could argue that the IRA terrorists were successful. After all, peace talks carried on after Brighton, the peace process developed, and today we have a degree of self-rule in Ulster. However, Lord Tebbit says the early release of prisoners and Magee's visit as a guest to the House of Commons to speak in 2009 may well give inspiration to the next generation of terrorists, namely al-Qaeda.[2] Republicans always point out that they too had casualties of 'war', subject to shootings and bombing themselves, as well as claiming terrible treatment at the hands of the UK government. The UK government itself would argue that it was fighting terrorism.

Security is definitely tighter since Brighton. A new Security Council was created after the bombing to look after the safety of the Prime Minister and the Cabinet. It included army explosive experts, senior police officers and security officers. This was one of the main results of the Hoddinott Report into the security failings at Brighton in 1984. The bomb at Brighton turned from news into history very quickly, but another question that still remains unanswered is who ordered the bombing? If Magee was the 'monkey', as Lord Tebbit says, will top-secret documents released in years to come finally tell us the name of the organ grinder? We can all take an educated guess as to who that might be, but maybe it's a name that will be a complete surprise to us all. To this day Patrick Magee refuses to disclose operational details of the bombing. When I asked him about those above him who ordered the attack and why he was chosen to carry it out, he answered very candidly and plausibly that he may well not have been privy to those decisions about why he was chosen and that he may have been the only one free at the time. Magee forgot to add here that he was known for his knowledge of explosives. In addition, Magee claims that giving details of the attack would only give offence to the victims.

At the end of September 2009 Labour caused outrage by inviting former IRA Commander, later Deputy First Minister of Northern Ireland, Martin McGuinness, to its conference in Brighton. One newspaper insisted that McGuinness showed no remorse for the bombing. The Northern Ireland Secretary Shaun Woodward and Business Secretary Lord Mandleson attended a breakfast meeting with Martin McGuinness at the conference, where he was asked if his past would ever be revealed. McGuinness said:

> I certainly think that if all of us were to talk about our past then we could actually make the situation for our political associates more difficult. I'm not prepared to do that at this stage. At some stage in the future all of my past will be before the general public. There are ways and means of doing that, but I am not ashamed of my past.[3]

Lord Tebbit described McGuinness as a terrorist and says he has no remorse. Tebbit argues that the UK, together with the United States, is engaged in the war against terror, and that we should look in our own backyard first. Or perhaps only the bomber Patrick Magee knows the identity of the man (or woman) who ordered the bombing. If that is the case, unless he reveals what he knows, these intimate parts of history may be lost forever. Tebbit says it is not just the names of the Brighton bombing ringleaders that need to come out, but he says former IRA godfathers now living in freedom at the tax payers' expense have to say where all the 'disappeared' victims in Ireland have been buried.[4]

Perhaps Magee's refusal to spill the beans on his former IRA commanders, coupled with hardly anything being written about the bombing on either political side, has created a degree of mystery surrounding Brighton. The emphasis seems to have been on Magee's desire to talk publicly about peace and reconciliation, rather than the unsolved past, which perhaps has not helped. How can we help the future, if we cannot heal the past? Politicians seem to want to forget Brighton, or not give it any publicity. Taking all this into account, the Brighton bombing has almost been swept under the carpet. It is with this in mind that I hope this book has highlighted some important historical questions.

Re-building the Grand Hotel

The hotel was rebuilt using reinforced concrete, partly because it is a material that can be constructed in a variety of shapes, so it could match the required form of construction of the building. A steel frame would have been difficult to get dimensionally right and in 1984–5 the engineers working on the Grand were concerned that the distance to span, particularly at high levels, would be very difficult to measure and accurately fit a steel frame into. Steel bars and reinforced concrete could cater for the size of the hole to be reconstructed. Today, the Grand Hotel remains a dominant physical Victorian feature on the town's seafront, with no evidence of the devastation of 1984. The interior was slightly redesigned in the rebuild so that the old Room 629 does not even exist.

Terrorist attacks such as Brighton have changed strength requirements for buildings that might be targets. When Heathrow's Terminal 5 was built no areas were closed in until authorities had checked that there were no concealments. A lot of the temporary bridges designed for the London 2012 Olympics had to be capable of withstanding an attack by a rogue vehicle.

What If?

Counterfactual history asks how history might have changed one way or another if something did not happen the way that it did. It is a method of evaluating the historical value and importance of a particular event. Its speculative nature and analytical positioning helps the historian develop an enquiring mind. However, there are many critics of this style. It is relatively new, although evidence exists from the 1930s and even a little from Victorian times, and a real debate has not yet developed. It does make history entertaining. In school history lessons, if you ask uninspired students 'what if Hitler had won the war' or 'what if William, Duke of Normandy had lost the Battle of Hastings', you will almost always get a response, especially if you tell them that they would now be speaking German. Lord Stockton's views (he was in the Grand that night but left early) that Kinnock would have become Prime Minister and there would have been no Tony Blair, perhaps no Iraq war, is a fascinating insight into how one event can change our entire history.

Appendix 1

Fire Brigade Personnel and Fire Stations Involved in the Brighton Incident

The table below lists brigade personnel, above the rank of Leading Fireman, who attended before the STOP message.

Name	Rank	Attached to Station
E.H. Whitaker	CFO	Brigade HQ
P.R. Rodgers	DCO	Brigade HQ
R. Stevenson	ACO	Brigade HQ
J. Kellett	SDO	Brigade HQ
R. Grainger	DO	Brigade HQ
B. Perkins	SDO	A Division HQ
R. Hull	DO	A Division HQ
R. Hill	DO	A Division HQ
R. Hayto	DO	A Division HQ
G. Hammond	DO	A Division HQ
W. Rigby	ADO	A Division HQ
T. McKinley	ADO	A Division HQ
F. Bishop	Stn O	Preston Circus
A. Cager	Stn O	Roedean
C. Findlay	Stn O	Hove
S. Webb	Stn O	Newhaven
J. Sivell	Stn O	Seaford
M. Broadway	Stn O	Barcombe
M. Denman	DO	A Division HQ
P. McGregor	Stn O	Worthing
R. Stevens	Stn O	Burgess Hill
G. Dunn	Stn O	Keymer
R. Brittan	Stn O	Shoreham
I. Henley	Stn O	Burgess Hill

The following fire stations assisted after the Brighton explosion:

Preston Circus
Roedean
Hove
Lewes
Newhaven
Seaford
Barcombe
Eastbourne
Uckfield
Shireham
Burgess Hill
Worthing
Horsham
Keymer

Appendix 2

A Brief Timeline of the Troubles

30 January 1972 – Bloody Sunday
Fourteen people were killed and thirteen injured in Derry after British paratroopers opened fire during a march against internment and the ban on marches. A section of protestors and observers confronted soldiers manning the barricade.

1972 – Direct Rule from Westminster Imposed
The Northern Ireland government was suspended in March and Northern Ireland came under Westminster rule. 'No-go' areas set up in 1969 were dismantled and the IRA responded by stepping up its violent activity.

5 October 1974
Four off-duty soldiers and a civilian died and forty-four people were injured in the Guildford pub bombings by the Provisional IRA.

29 November 1974 – The Prevention of Terrorism Act
This Act was introduced after a series of IRA bombings across the UK and Ireland. Suspects could now be detained without charge for up to seven days.

20 December 1975
The UDA bombed Biddy Mulligan's pub in the Kilburn area of London. Five people were injured.

15 May 1976
Five Catholic civilians killed and many injured by two Ulster Volunteer Force bomb attacks in Belfast and Charlemont.

30 March 1979

The Irish National Liberation Army (INLA) claimed responsibility for the killing of Airey Neave after a car bomb exploded under his car as he drove out of the Palace of Westminster car park.

1980s – Hunger Strikes and Protest

After 'special prisoner status' had been removed by the UK government in 1976, dirty protests, blanket protests and hunger strikes followed. Bobby Sands was the first hunger striker in 1981. He died, as did nine other hunger strikers.

10 October 1981

An IRA bomb went off outside the Chelsea Barracks, London. Two died and thirty-nine people were injured.

20 July 1982

The Hyde Park and Regent's Park bombings by the IRA killed eleven members of the Household Cavalry and Royal Green Jackets.

17 December 1983

Six people were killed and ninety were wounded after a bomb went off at Harrods department store in London.

12 October 1984

The Brighton hotel bombing resulted in the deaths of five people and more than thirty injuries.

15 November 1985 – Anglo-Irish Agreement Signed

Unionists were outraged that the Agreement gave Dublin a say over the affairs of Northern Ireland and the Agreement was never fully implemented, despite peace talks involving both sides.

7 February 1991
The IRA launched three mortar shells into the garden at 10 Downing Street.

10 April 1992
A large bomb exploded in the City of London, killing three people. The Semtex bomb was contained in a large white truck.

15 December 1993 – Downing Street Declaration
This stated that representatives of different groups should meet to discuss a solution to the ongoing Troubles. Sinn Fein was invited to take part on the condition that IRA violence was stopped. The IRA declared a ceasefire in 1994; Loyalist groups followed.

15 June 1996
An IRA bomb damaged the Arndale Shopping Centre in Manchester, injuring 206 people.

1996 – Peace Talks
American Senator George Mitchell chaired talks. He proposed that disarmament should start but this led to a stalling of the talks. Violence resumed after the IRA broke its ceasefire.

10 April 1998 – Belfast (Good Friday) Agreement
In 1997 Sinn Fein was invited to take part in peace talks on condition that a six-week IRA ceasefire had been observed. After many months of discussion a settlement was reached on Good Friday, 1998.

Appendix 3

Quotes About the Brighton Bombing

'The Brighton bombing was the most extraordinary event that you could imagine; an attempt to blow up as much of the Government as they could and to do so in a very public situation.'

Leon Brittan, Home Secretary in 1984,
Channel 4 documentary The Brighton Bombing, *2003*

'A cowardly, evil act that damaged families and individuals in a way that was utterly, utterly impossible to justify.'

John Gummer, Conservative Party Chairman in 1984,
Channel 4 documentary The Brighton Bombing, *2003*

'An attack on one is an attack on all, and an attack on all is an attack on one.'

Lord Elton, House of Lords, 22 October 1984

A nurse asks Norman Tebbit being stretchered into hospital, 'Are you allergic to anything?' Tebbit replied, 'Yes, bombs!'

'Pat [Patrick Magee] was an honourable IRA volunteer and cannot be faulted for his beliefs indeed militarily Brighton was a very clever and brave operation.'

anon., Youtube, 2009

'The message I get from this is that terrorism works. I fear as we enter a new era of insurgency this sort of message will have a much bloodier price.'

anon., Youtube, 2009

Notes

Chapter 1

1. Brian Harrison, 'Neave, Airey Middleton Sheffield (1916–1979)', *Oxford Dictionary of National Biography* (Oxford: Oxford University Press, 2004); online edition, January 2011, http://www.oxforddnb.com/view/article/31488; accessed 15 March 2014.
2. C. Collins, 'Thatcher, Sir Denis, First Baronet (1915–2003)', *Oxford Dictionary of National Biography* (Oxford: Oxford University Press, 2007); online edition, January 2011, http://www.oxforddnb.com/view/article/90063; accessed 15 March 2014.
3. *Ibid.*
4. http://openplaques.org/people/3042; accessed 20 February 2014.

Chapter 4

1. J. Blundell, *Margaret Thatcher: A Portrait of the Iron Lady* (New York: Algora Publishing, 2008), p. 133 .
2. Channel 4 documentary *The Brighton Bombing*, executive producer John Bridcut, 2003.
3. *Ibid.*
4. http://www.dannymorrison.com/wp-content/dannymorrisonarchive/216.htm; accessed 1 June 2014.

Chapter 5

1. Arwel Ellis Owen, *The Anglo-Irish Agreement. The First Three Years* (Cardiff: University of Wales Press, 1994), p. 43.
2. *Ibid.*, p. 33.
3. http://hansard.millbanksystems.com/commons/1998/apr/22/northern-ireland-election-bill#S6CV0310P0_19980422_HOC_479; accessed 26 June 2014.
4. *Ibid.*

Chapter 7

1. P. Gurney, *Braver Men Walk Away* (London: HarperCollins, 1993), pp. 6–8.
2. Private correspondence with Lord Jenkin, 28 July 2013.
3. http://dictionary.reference.com; accessed 5 December 2013.

4. *Ibid.*; accessed 5 January 2014.
5. http://dictionary.cambridge.org; accessed 5 December 2013.
6. http://www.oxforddictionaries.com; accessed 5 December 2013.
7. http://www.fbi.gov/about-us, Definitions of Terrorism in the U.S. Code; accessed 5 December 2013.
8. J.L. Stump and P. Dixit, *Critical Terrorism Studies* (London: Routledge, 2012).
9. S. O'Callaghan, *The Informer* (London: Corgi, 1999).

Chapter 9
1. Incident Report, Sussex Fire & Rescue, p. 5.
2. K. Hughes, interview with George Hammond (Sussex Fire & Rescue), 20 November 2009.
3. Channel 4 documentary *The Brighton Bombing*, executive producer John Bridcut, 2003.
4. www.fireservice.co.uk, Famous Incidents, 'The Brighton Bombing, 12 Oct 1984'; accessed 19 May 2014.
5. J. Fryer, 'The Cuddly Side to the Chingford Skinhead', *Daily Mail*, 18 April 2014, in http://www.dailymail.co.uk/news/article-2608128/The-cuddly-Chingford-Skinhead; accessed 26 May 2014.
6. K. Hughes, interview with George Hammond (Sussex Fire & Rescue), 20 November 2009.
7. *Ibid.*
8. D. Hughes, 'The Brighton Bombing', *Daily Telegraph*, September 2009.
9. K. Hughes, interview with George Hammond (Sussex Fire & Rescue), 20 November 2009.
10. M. Garnett and I. Aitken, *Splendid! Splendid! The Authorised Biography of Willie Whitelaw* (London: Pimlico Books, 2002), p. 310.
11. Channel 4 documentary *The Brighton Bombing*, executive producer John Bridcut, 2003.
12. 'Thatcher interview', *A4 Plus*, J. Tagholm (ed.), Thames Television, 1984.
13. D. McKittrick and D. McVea, *Making Sense of the Troubles* (London: Penguin Books, 2001), p. 162.

Chapter 10
1. Incident Report, Sussex Fire & Rescue.
2. Interview with Simon Parr, 30 April 2014, via email.
3. www.fireservice.co.uk, Famous Incidents, 'The Brighton Bombing, 12 Oct 1984'; accessed 19 May 2014.
4. 'Sir Gordon Shattock', 2 May 2010, http://www.telegraph.co.uk/news/obituaries/politics-obituaries/7669698/Sir-Gordon-Shattock.html; accessed 19 May 2014.
5. Incident Report, Sussex Fire & Rescue, Appendix 'H'.

6. Channel 4 documentary *The Brighton Bombing*, executive producer John Bridcut, 2003.
7. *Daily Mail* chatroom; accessed 1 May 2014.
8. Incident Report, Sussex Fire & Rescue, section 8.24.

Chapter 11
1. D. McKittrick, 'The Brighton Bomb and Mrs Thatcher' April 2013, via http://eamonnmallie.com/2013/04/the-brighton-bomb-and-mrs-thatcher; accessed 20 July 2014.
2. Telephone interview with Michael Dobbs, 2 June 2014.
3. R.W. Jones, 'Margaret Thatcher 1925–2013: War with the IRA and Surviving the Brighton Bombing', 9 April 2013, http://www.mirror.co.uk/news/uk-news/margaret-thatcher-dead-war-ira; accessed 29 June 2014.
4. Margaret Thatcher's Speech to Conservative Party Conference, 12 October 1984, http://www.margaretthatcher.org/document/105763; accessed 2 April 2014.
5. Harvey Thomas MSS; copy now in Thatcher MSS, via margaretthatcher.org; accessed 28 June 2014.
6. http://www.britishpoliticalspeech.org/speech-archive.htm?speech=130; accessed 28 June 2014.
7. M. Thatcher, *The Downing Street Years* (London: HarperCollins, 1995), pp. 379–83.
8. hansard.millbanksystems.com/lords/1984/oct/16/grand-hotel-brighton-bomb-explosion; accessed 25 June 2014.

Chapter 12
1. Northern Ireland: Reagan letter to Thatcher, Brighton bomb sympathies, Reagan Library: NSA Head of State File (Box 36), declassified 2000, 1984 Oct 12, via http://www.margaretthatcher.org; accessed 14 February 2014.
2. 'Recommended telephone call', 12 October 1984, http://www.margaretthatcher.org/document/109352; accessed 21 June 2014.
3. Speech at Lord Mayor's Banquet, 12 November 1984, via http://www.margaretthatcher.org; accessed 16 February 2014.
4. David Bret, *Morrissey* (London: Robson Books, 2000).
5. http://www.plyrics.com/a/angelicupstarts.html; accessed 25 May 2014.
6. http://hansard.millbanksystems.com/commons/1984/dec/06/business-of-the-house#S6CV0069P0_19841206_HOC_167; accessed 25 June 2014.

Chapter 13
1. K. Toolis, 'Brighton, A Two Way Trial of Bungling and Incompetence', *Fortnight* magazine (Belfast: Fortnight Publications Ltd, 7 July–7 September 1986), p. 14, via Jstor; accessed 17 December 2009.

Chapter 14

1. McKittrick and McVea, *Making Sense of the Troubles*, p. 162.
2. C. Kennedy-Pipe, *The Origins of the Present Troubles in Northern Ireland* (Harlow: Longman, 1997), p. 121.
3. K. Hughes, interview with Norman Tebbit at the House of Lords, 11 November 2009.
4. Private correspondence with Patrick Jenkin, 28 July 2013.
5. K. Hughes, interview with Lord Stockton, 12 January 2010.
6. Private correspondence with Douglas Hurd, 16 March 2010.
7. M. Holland, 'Ireland Blasts Back', *New Statesman*, 19 October 1985, p. 3.
8. K. Toolis, 'Into an Anglo-Irish Impasse', *Fortnight* (Belfast: Fortnight Publications Ltd, November 1984), p. 3.
9. M. Stuart, *Douglas Hurd the Public Servant, an Authorised Biography* (Edinburgh: Mainstream, 1998), p. 140.
10. J. Lyons, 'Brighton Bomb that almost killed Margaret Thatcher came close to scuppering Northern Ireland peace talks', 3 January 1014, http://www.mirror.co.uk/news/uk-news/brighton-bomb-killed-margaret-thatcher-2982073; accessed 1 March 2014.
11. http://hansard.millbanksystems.com/commons/1998/apr/22/northern-ireland-election-bill#S6CV0310P0_19980422_HOC_479; accessed 30 April 2014.
12. *Ibid.*; accessed 1 May 2014.
13. *Ibid.*
14. HC Deb 26 November 1985, vol. 87 cc747-828, http://hansard.millbanksystems.com/commons/1985/nov/26/anglo-irish-agreement#S6CV0087P0_19851126_HOC_298; accessed 5 July 2014.
15. *Ibid.*; accessed 2 May 2014.

Chapter 15

1. Cabinet meeting minutes, The National Archives, Kew, TNA ref. CAB 128/79/10.
2. Kennedy-Pipe, *The Origins of the Present Troubles in Northern Ireland*, p. 122.
3. Jones, 'Margaret Thatcher 1925–2013: War with the IRA and Surviving the Brighton Bombing', 9 April 2013, http://www.mirror.co.uk/news/uk-news/margaret-thatcher-dead-war-ira; accessed 29 June 2014.
4. Henry Patterson, *Ireland Since 1939: The Persistence of Conflict* (London: Penguin, 2007).
5. R. Wynne Jones, 'Margaret Thatcher 1925–2013: War with the IRA and surviving the Brighton bombing', 9 April 2013, http://www.mirror.co.uk/news/uk-news/margaret-thatcher-dead-war-ira-1820429; accessed 2 May 2014.
6. G. Howe, *Conflict of Loyalty* (London: Macmillan, 1994), p. 419.

7. Powell minute to Armstrong ('Anglo-Irish Relations: Northern Ireland') PREM19/1288   f149,   http://www.margaretthatcher.org/document/134210; accessed 2 July 2014.
8. Holland, 'Ireland Blasts Back', p. 3.
9. Private correspondence with Douglas Hurd, 16 March 2010.
10. K. Hughes, interview with Lord Stockton, 12 January 2010.
11. everything2.com/title/Brighton+Bombing; accessed 1 February 2014.
12. Channel 4 documentary, *The Brighton Bombing*, 1998.
13. *Ibid.*
14. Tebbit, *Upwardly Mobile*, p. 229.
15. *Ibid.*, p. 232.
16. Private correspondence with Douglas Hurd, 16 March 2010.
17. G. Davidson Smith, *Combatting Terrorism* (London: Routledge, 1990), p. 196.

Chapter 16
1. hansard.millbanksystems.com/lords/1984/oct/16/grand-hotel-brighton-bomb-explosion; accessed 25 June 2014.
2. *Ibid.*; accessed 1 July 2014.
3. 'Grand Hotel, Brighton: Bomb Explosion', House of Lords, 16 October 1984 vol. 455 cc884-8, http://hansard.millbanksystems.com/lords/1984/oct/16/grand-hotel-brighton-bomb-explosion; accessed 29 April 2014.
4. Thatcher, *The Downing Street Years*, pp. 379–83.
5. www.margaretthatcher.org/speeches; accessed 16 March 2014.
6. K. Hughes, interview with Lord Stockton, 12 January 2010.
7. Private correspondence with Lord Jenkin, 28 July 2013.
8. *TV-AM* interview with Margaret Thatcher, June 1985, via Youtube; accessed 30 December 2013.
9. 'The Margaret Thatcher I knew: 20 personal insights', 8 April 2013, http://www.theguardian.com/politics/interactive/2013/apr/08/margaret-thatcher-i-knew; accessed March 2014.
10. L. Murawiec, 'After the Brighton bombing: Who will end Britain's political paralysis?', *EIR*, vol. 11, no. 43, 6 November 1984.
11. T. Koolis, *Rebel Hearts, Journeys within the IRA's Soul* (London: Picador Books, 2000), p. 349.
12. www.spiked-online.com; accessed 23 February 2014.

Chapter 17
1. D. Moller, 'Heroes of the Brighton Bombing', *Reader's Digest* (London: 1985), pp. 163–76
2. Thatcher, *The Downing Street Years*, p. 379.
3. P. Chalk, *Encyclopaedia of Terrorism* (Santa Barbara: ABC-CLIO, 2012).

4. http://books.google.co.uk/books?id=czK7lIU7m1oC&printsec=frontcov er&dq=Peter+chalk&hl=en&sa=X&ei=hprYU8a-GIbtPJWggZAF&ved= 0CCwQ6AEwAQ#v=onepage&q=cellophane&f=false; accessed 18 April 2014.
5. K. Hughes, interview with structural engineer Marek Kubik, 20 March 2010.
6. *Ibid.*
7. Interview with engineer Jon Orrell, 20 January 2014.
8. Gurney, *Braver Men Walk Away*, p. 171.
9. *Ibid.*
10. *Ibid.*

Chapter 18

1. M. Portillo, 'The bomb that set Labour and Tory apart', September 2004, http://www.michaelportillo.co.uk/articles/art_nipress/labour.htm, quoting *Sunday Times* article; accessed 1 June 2014.
2. *Ibid.*
3. Hansard, HL Deb 16 October 1984, vol. 455 cc884-8, http://hansard. millbanksystems.com/lords/1984/oct/16/grand-hotel-brighton-bomb-explosion; accessed 24 June 2014.
4. G. McGladdery, *The Provisional IRA in England: the Bombing Campaign 1973–1997* (County Kildare: Irish Academic Press, 2006), p. 100.
5. http://hansard.millbanksystems.com/commons; accessed 1 May 2014.
6. *Ibid.*
7. *Ibid.*
8. *Ibid.*
9. *Ibid.*
10. *Ibid.*
11. *Ibid.*
12. Davidson Smith, *Combatting Terrorism*, p. 196.
13. *Ibid.*
14. The *Tablet, The International Catholic News Weekly*, 18 September 2004, p. 27, via archive.thetablet.co.uk; accessed 15 August 2014.
15. http://www.sinnfein.ie/contents/20204; accessed 3 July 2014.
16. C. Andrew, *Defence of the Realm* (London: Penguin, 2010).
17. Speech to Conservative Party Conference, 14 October 1988, http://www. margaretthatcher.org/document/107352; accessed 13 June 2014.
18. 'Mrs Thatcher: The Unshakeable PM', *Birmingham Post*, 29 October 1984, http://www.margaretthatcher.org; accessed 13 February 2014.
19. 'Thatcher interview', *A4 Plus*, J. Tagholm (ed.), Thames Television, 1984.
20. Kevin Toolis, *Rebel Hearts: Journeys within the IRA's Soul* (London: Picador Books, 2000), p. 277.
21. *Ibid.*, p. 279.

22. C. Walker, *The Prevention of Terrorism in British Law, 2nd Edition* (Manchester: Manchester University Press, 1992), p. 245.

23. K. Hughes, interview with George Hammond (Sussex Fire & Rescue), 20 November 2009.

24. Interview with Simon Parr, 30 April 2014, via email.

25. *Ibid.*

26. Speech to Conservative Party Conference, 14 October 1988, http://www.margaretthatcher.org/document/107352; accessed 20 June 2014.

27. www.parliament.uk/parliamentary_publications_and_archives; accessed 2 December 2009.

28. Gurney, *Braver men Walk Away*, p. 172.

Chapter 19

1. http://theforgivenessproject.com/stories/jo-berry-pat-magee-england; accessed 1 March 2014.

2. *Ibid.*

3. P. Good, 'Controversy Over Event in London Marking 25th Anniversary of the Brighton Bomb', 20 April 2010, http://theforgivenessproject.com/controversy-over-event-in-london; accessed 12 February 2014.

4. G. Levy and N. Kafri , 'The IRA Veteran', 2013, via Haaretz.com; accessed 10 July 2014.

5. J. Moore and P. Nero, *History's Narrowest Escapes* (Stroud: The History Press, 2013), p. 191.

6. Lynne J. Cameron, *Metaphor and Reconciliation* (London: Routledge, 2011), Preface.

7. http://theforgivenessproject.com/stories/jo-berry-pat-magee-england; accessed 1 March 2014.

8. *Ibid.*

9. Jo Berry, founder, buildingbridgesforpeace.org; accessed 24 June 2014.

10. http://www.youtube.com/watch?v=HN3A7iZYISM; accessed 12 March 2014.

11. http://theforgivenessproject.com/about-us/testimonials; accessed 1 July 2014.

12. Telephone interview with Simon Fanshawe, 14 June 2014.

13. S. Fanshawe, 'Thomas the Tank Engine and treading on eggs shells', 13 October 2011, http://simonfanshawe.com; accessed 31 May 2014.

14. M. Allinson, 'Peace in Northern Ireland: A model of success?', 15 August 2012, http://www.aljazeera.com/indepth/opinion/2012/08/20128129222 3454712/html; accessed 4 July 2014.

15. *Ibid.*

16. C. Hall, 'Brighton bombing 25 years on: Making friends with my father's killer', 10 October 2009, http://www.theguardian.com; accessed 20 November 2013.

17. 'Brighton bomber Patrick Magee remains defiant during House of Commons visit', 14 October 2009, http://www.mirror.co.uk/news/uk-news/brighton-bomber; accessed 12 December 2013.

18. C. Gysin, 'Killer in the Commons: IRA man Patrick Magee planted the Brighton bomb. Now he's invited to talk to MPs … about forgiveness', 13 October 2009, http://www.dailymail.co.uk/newsCommons-IRA'; accessed 1 January 2013.

19. 'Keep the Brighton Bomber out of Parliament', 11 October 2009; http://www.heraldscotland.com/news/politics/keep-the-brighton-bomber-out-of-parliament; accessed 30 January 2014.

20. 'Brighton bomber: I don't want forgiveness but I feel regret', *Belfast Telegraph*, 14 October 2009, http://www.belfasttelegraph.co.uk/news/local-national/brighton-bomber; accessed 30 December 2013.

21. *Sun*, 14 October 2009, p. 2.

22. 'Four PSNI officers injured during ex-IRA bomber protest', 31 January 2014, http://www.bbc.co.uk/news/uk.; accessed 31 May 2014.

23. C. Hope and J. Kirkup, 'Queen tells state banquet attended by Martin McGuinness that goal of peaceful British-Irish relations "within reach"', http://www.telegraph.co.uk/news/uknews/queen-elizabeth-II; accessed 8 April 2014.

24. Telephone interview with Michael Dobbs, 2 June 2014.

25. Private correspondence with Lord Jenkin, 28 July 2013.

26. K. Hughes, interview with Patrick Magee, 18 November 2009.

27. G. Levy and N. Kafri , 'The IRA Veteran', via Haaretz.com; accessed 10 July 2014.

28. K. Hughes, interview with Patrick Magee, 18 November 2009.

29. *Daily Mail*, 13 October 2009, p. 4.

30. G. Levy and N. Kafri , 'The IRA Veteran', via Haaretz.com; accessed 10 July 2014.

31. M. Lawson, 'And I thought we were friends, Tony', 13 September 2004, http://www.theguardian.com/media/2004/sep/13/broadcasting.bbc1; accessed 9 June 2014.

32. K. Hughes, interview with Patrick Magee, 18 November 2009.

33. S. Elworthy and F. Cerletti (eds), *Unarmed Heroes: the Courage to Go Beyond Violence* (London: Claireview Books, 2004), p. 24.

34. 'America in the World', 13 March 2005, http://henryjacksonsociety.org/2005/03/13/opening-editorial-america-in-the-world; accessed 12 June 2016.

35. M. Toaldo, *The Origins of the US War on Terror: Lebanon, Libya and American*, (Abingdon: Routledge, 2013), p. 103.

36. *Ibid.*, p. 106.

37. K. Hughes, interview with Patrick Magee, 18 November 2009.

38. *An Phoblacht Republican News*, 14 October 1984, front page.
39. K. Hughes, interview with Lord Tebbit at the House of Lords, 11 November 2009.
40. Holland, 'Ireland Blasts Back', *New Statesman*, 19 October 1985, p. 3.
41. K. Hughes, interview with Patrick Magee, 18 November 2009.
42. *Ibid*.
43. *Ibid*.
44. *Ibid*.
45. Channel 4 documentary *The Brighton Bombing*, executive producer John Bridcut, 2003.

Chapter 20
1. Tebbit, *Upwardly Mobile*, p. 236.
2. K. Hughes, interview with George Hammond (Sussex Fire & Rescue), 20 November 2009.
3. K. Hughes, interview with Patrick Magee, 18 November 2009.
4. Observations of journalist Mark Lawson on *The Hunt for the Bomber* (broadcast 14 September 2004) in 'And I thought we were friends, Tony', 13 September 2004, http://www.theguardian.com/media/2004/sep/13/broadcasting.bbc1; accessed 15 August 2014.
5. K. Hughes, interview with Lord Tebbit at the House of Lords, 11 November 2009.
6. *Ibid*.

Chapter 21
1. http://hansard.millbanksystems.com/commons/1988/oct/19/broadcasting-and-terrorism; accessed 28 June 2014.
2. *Ibid*.
3. *Ibid*.
4. *Ibid*.
5. *Ibid*.
6. *Ibid*.
7. *Ibid*.
8. R. Moseley, 'On British TV, IRA is Speechless – Leaders' Voices Not Allowed In Broadcasts', December 1993, http://articles.chicagotribune.com/1993-12-25/news/9312250076_1_northern-ireland-gerry-adams-british-tv; accessed 29 June 2014.

Chapter 22
1. See the Bibliography for individual book details.
2. M. Heseltine, *Life in the Jungle, My Autobiography* (London: Coronet Books, 2000), p. 280.

3. Howe, *Conflict of Loyalty*, p. 419.
4. S. Hoggart, 'Brighton Rocked', *Spectator*, 17 May 2003, p. 78, http:// archive.spectator.co.uk/article/17th-may-2003/78/brighton-rocked; accessed 9 June 2014.

Chapter 23
1. M. Mansergh, 'Striking a balance: The Northern Ireland peace process', 1999, http://www.c-r.org/accord-article/early-stages-irish-peace-process-1999; accessed 19 May 2014.

Conclusion
1. K. Hughes, interview with Lord Stockton, 12 January 2010.
2. K. Hughes, interview with Lord Tebbit at the House of Lords, 11 November 2009.
3. BBC News online, October 2009; accessed 20 February 2014.
4. Norman Tebbit, 'Will we ever learn from the Brighton bomb?', *Daily Telegraph*, 12 October 2009.

Bibliography

Primary Sources

Hammond, George, fireman, one-to-one interview, 5 November 2009

Hansard, HL Deb 16 October 1984, vol. 455 cc884-8, hansard.millbank systems.com/lords/1984/oct/16/grand-hotel-brighton-bomb-explosion; accessed 25 June 2014

http://hansard.millbanksystems.com/commons/1985/jan/22/brighton-bombing-hoddinott-report; accessed 2 December 2009

http://hansard.millbanksystems.com/lords; accessed 12 January 2010

http://hansard.millbanksystems.com/lords/1984/oct/16/grand-hotel-brighton-bomb-explosion; accessed 24 June 2014

HC Deb 6 December 1984, vol. 69 cc499-507, http://hansard.millbank systems.com/commons/1984/dec/06/business-of-the-house#S6CV 0069P0_19841206_HOC_167; accessed 25 June 2014

HC Deb 22 April 1998, vol. 310 cc847-89, http://hansard.millbanksystems. com/commons/1998/apr/22/northern-ireland-election-bill#S6CV0310P0_19980422_HOC_479; accessed 26 June 2014

HC Deb 19 October 1988, vol. 138 cc893-903, http://hansard.millbanksystems. com/commons/1988/oct/19/broadcasting-and-terrorism; accessed 2 December 2009

Hurd, Douglas, now Lord Hurd, former Northern Ireland Secretary, private letter to the author, February 2010

Kubik, Marek, researcher in civil engineering at the TSBE Centre, in Reading, email interview, February 2010

Lawton, Frank, PO Box 196, MONTROSE, VIC, 3765, Independent expert on forensics, ballistics, shootings, firearms, ammunition, gunshot residue, explosives and bombings, email interview, February 2010

Magee, Patrick, one-to-one interview, 7 November 2009

http://news.bbc.co.uk/onthisday; accessed 1 January 2010

PA Photos/via BBC News website; accessed 25 November 2009

parliament.uk/parliamentary_publications_and_archives/parliamentary_archives/enquiry_ser; accessed 2 December 2009

Parr, Simon, former Sussex Police officer, interviewed via email, 30 April 2014

Powell minute to Armstrong, 'Anglo-Irish Relations: Northern Ireland', PREM19/1288 f149, http://www.margaretthatcher.org/document/134210; accessed 2 July 2014

http://www.sinnfein.ie/what-sinn-fein-stands-for; accessed 15 July 2014

Stockton, Lord, one-to-one interview, 12 January 2010

Sussex Fire & Rescue Incident Report, 1985/6

Tebbit, Lord, one-to-one interview, 11 November 2009

Secondary Sources

Allinson, M., 'Peace in Northern Ireland: A model of success?', 15 August 2012, http://www.aljazeera.com/indepth/opinion/2012/08/201281292223 454712.html; accessed 4 July 2014

An Phoblacht Republican News, 14 October 1984, front cover

http://www.ark.ac.uk/elections/ggfa.htm; accessed 17 June 2014

Arwel Ellis, Owen, *The Anglo-Irish Agreement. The First Three Years*, Cardiff: University of Wales Press, 1994

BBC Parliament Channel interview with author Christopher Andrew, broadcast 14 April 2010, 8.45a.m., London, discussing MI5 issues and his book on the Secret Service, *The Defence of the Realm*, London: Allen Lane, 2009

Blundell, J., *Margaret Thatcher: A Portrait of the Iron Lady*, New York: Algora Publishing, 2008

'Brighton: Bomb Aftermath', *Channel Four News*, broadcast 18 October 1984 (taken from NFO Collection)

The Brighton Bombing, Channel Four documentaries, London, 1998; accessed via youtube.com, 13 January 2010

http://www.britishpoliticalspeech.org/speech-archive.htm?speech=130; accessed 28 June 2014

buildingbridgesforpeace.org; accessed 24 June 2014

http://cain.ulst.ac.uk/events/assembly1982/chronology.htm; accessed 1 October 2009

Cameron, Lynne J. *Metaphor and Reconciliation*, London: Routledge, 2011

http://www.c-r.org/accord-article/early-stages-irish-peace-process-1999; 17 June 2014.

Daily Mail, 1 October 2009, 13 October 2009

dailytelegraph.co.uk, 11 October 2009; accessed 13 October 2010

Davidson Smith, G., *Combatting Terrorism*, London: Routledge, 1990

'The Day the Troubles Began', 2014, http://www.bbc.co.uk/history/events/day_troubles_began; accessed 5 May 2014

Elworthy, S. and Cerletti, F. (eds), *Unarmed Heroes: the Courage to go Beyond Violence*, London: Claireview Books, 2004

everything2.com/title/Brighton+Bombing; accessed 16 January 2010

Fanshawe, S., 'Thomas the Tank Engine and treading on eggs shells', 13 October 2011, http://simonfanshawe.com; accessed 31 May 2014

Fitzsimmons, Paul A., *Independence for Northern Ireland, Why and How*, Washington DC: The Juris Press, 1993

Fryer, J., 'The Cuddly Side to the Chingford Skinhead', *Daily Mail*, 18 April 2014, http://www.dailymail.co.uk/news/article-2608128/The-cuddly-Chingford-Skinhead; accessed 26 May 2014

Gainesville Sun, Florida, 15 October 1984; accessed via Gainesville.com, 2 February 2010

Garnett, M. and Aitken, I., *Splendid! Splendid! The Authorised Biography of Willie Whitelaw*, London: Pimlico Books, 2002

Gurney, P., *Braver Men Walk Away*, London: HarperCollins, 1993

Heath, E., *The Course of My Life: My Autobiography*, London: Hodder & Stoughton, 1998

Heseltine, M., *Life in the Jungle, My Autobiography*, London: Coronet Books, 2000

Hoggart, S., 'Brighton Rocked', *Spectator*, 17 May 2003, p. 78

http://archive.spectator.co.uk/article/17th-may-2003/78/brighton-rocked; accessed 9 June 2014

Holland, M., 'Ireland Blasts Back', *New Statesman*, 19 October 1985; accessed via Jstor

Howe, G., *Conflict of Loyalty*, London: Macmillan, 1994

Hughes, D., 'Brighton Bombing: Daily Telegraph Journalist Recalls'; accessed via dailytelegraph.com, 11 October 2009

Hurd, D., *Memoirs*, London: Abacus, 2004

Jones, R.W., 'Margaret Thatcher 1925–2013: War with the IRA and Surviving the Brighton Bombing', 9 April 2013, http://www.mirror.co.uk/news/uk-news/margaret-thatcher-dead-war-ira,ira; accessed 29 June 2014

Kennedy-Pipe, C., *The Origins of the Present Troubles in Northern Ireland*, Harlow: Longman, 1997

Lawson, M., 'And I thought we were friends, Tony', 13 September 2004, http://www.theguardian.com/media/2004/sep/13/broadcasting.bbc1; accessed 9 June 2014

Levy, G. and Kafri, N., 'The IRA veteran and the daughter of a slain MP who preached peace to Israelis', *Haaretz*, 17 March 2013, http://www.haaretz.com/weekend/twilight-zone/the-ira; accessed 7 June 2014

londondrum.com/history/IRA-bombings; accessed 3 January 2010

McGladdery, G., *The Provisional IRA in England: the Bombing Campaign 1973–1997*, County Kildare: Irish Academic Press, 2006

McKittrick, David and McVea, D., *Making Sense of the Troubles*, London: Penguin Books, 2001

Major, J., *The Autobiography*, London: HarperCollins, 1999

Moller, D., 'Heroes of the Brighton Bombing', *Reader's Digest*, London, 1985

Moseley, R., 'On British TV, IRA is Speechless – Leaders' Voices Not Allowed In Broadcasts', December 1993, http://articles.chicagotribune.com/1993-12-25/news/9312250076_1_northern-ireland-gerry-adams-british-tv; accessed 29 June 2014

'Northern Ireland Timeline', May 2010, http://www.historyonthenet.com/Chronology/timelinenorthernireland.htm; accessed 18 May 2014

Nott, J., *Here Today, Gone Tomorrow: Recollections of an Errant Politician*, London: Politico, 2003

Parkinson, C., *Right at the Centre*, London: Weidenfeld & Nicolson, 1992

Patterson, H., *Ireland Since 1939: The Persistence of Conflict*, London: Penguin Books, 2006

http://www.sinnfein.ie/contents/20204; accessed 3 July 2014

'Sir Gordon Shattock', 2 May 2010, http://www.telegraph.co.uk/news/obituaries/politics-obituaries/7669698/Sir-Gordon-Shattock.html; accessed 19 May 2014

Stuart, M., *Douglas Hurd the Public Servant, an Authorised Biography*, Edinburgh: Mainstream, 1998

Sun, 14 October 2009, p. 2

Tebbit, N., *Upwardly Mobile*, London: Weidenfield & Nicolson, 1988

'Thatcher interview', *A4 Plus*, J. Tagholm (ed.), 1984, for Thames Television; accessed 21 June 2014

Thatcher, M., *The Downing Street Years*, London: HarperCollins, 1995

Toolis, K., *Rebel Hearts, Journeys within the IRA's Soul*, London: Picador Books, 2000

Toolis, K., 'Brighton, A Two Way Trial of Bungling and Incompetence', *Fortnight*, Belfast: Fortnight Publications Ltd, 7 July–7 September 1986, via Jstor; accessed 17 December 2009

Toolis, K., 'Into an Anglo-Irish Impasse?', *Fortnight*, Belfast: Fortnight Publications Ltd, November 1984

Walker, Dr C., *The Prevention of Terrorism in British Law, 2nd Edition*, Manchester: Manchester University Press, 1992

Wynne Jones, R., 'Margaret Thatcher 1925–2013: War with the IRA and surviving the Brighton bombing', 9 April 2013, http://www.mirror.co.uk/news/uk-news/margaret-thatcher-dead-war-ira-1820429; accessed 2 May 2014

http://www.youtube.com/watch?v=HN3A7iZYISM; accessed 20 May 2014.

'Four PSNI officers injured during ex-IRA bomber protest', 31 January 2014, http://www.bbc.co.uk/news/uk; accessed 31 May 2014

Index